I0148258

Pickett's Charge

General George Pickett

Pickett's Charge
The Great Confederate Attack at the Battle of
Gettysburg, July 3rd, 1863
ILLUSTRATED

Arthur Griffiths
James E. Crocker
LaSalle Corbell Pickett
James I. Metts
Helen D. Longstreet
James Longstreet
A Member of the Virginia Historical Society

LEONAUR

Pickett's Charge
The Great Confederate Attack at the Battle of Gettysburg, July 3rd, 1863
ILLUSTRATED
by Arthur Griffiths
James E. Crocker
LaSalle Corbell Pickett
James I. Metts
Helen D. Longstreet
James Longstreet
A Member of the Virginia Historical Society

FIRST EDITION

Leonaur is an imprint of Oakpast Ltd

Copyright in this form © 2017 Oakpast Ltd

ISBN: 978-1-78282-596-8 (hardcover)
ISBN: 978-1-78282-597-5 (softcover)

http://www.leonaur.com

Publisher's Notes

The views expressed in this book are not necessarily
those of the publisher.

Contents

An Overview of the Battle of Gettysburg: July 1st, 2nd, 3rd, 1863

By Arthur Griffiths

Gettysburg ranks with the battles that have decided the fate of empires. Had the issue been different the cause of the Confederacy would no doubt have triumphed and the United States have been split in twain. It was fought when the fortunes of the South were at their highest point. Recent victories at Fredericksburg and Chancellorsville had greatly raised their morale. Their army had been recruited and was reorganised under efficient and much trusted commanders; they were in a position to carry the war into the enemy's country, to invade the States still faithful to the Union, and threaten the Central Government at Washington. On the other hand, the Federals were weakened and dispirited. The withdrawal of many short-service men had greatly reduced their strength, and they had been but lately twice defeated in the open field. Had the Confederates won at Gettysburg, nothing could well have prevented their occupation of Pennsylvania and Maryland. Other far-reaching consequences all tending to the success of the rebellion were more than probable.

It was General Robert E. Lee, at that time the Confederate general-in-chief, who planned the operations that ended in the Battle of Gettysburg. Whatever his ultimate aim, no doubt his immediate object was the defence of Richmond, the Southern capital, by an offensive counter attack. His advance was a wide outflanking movement, a blow boldly and unexpectedly struck so far to the rear that the Federals must at once fall back. Thus Richmond would be immediately relieved, while other decisive results would in all probability follow.

A word or two first about Lee, that fine soldier whom his foes compared to Napoleon, declaring that his presence on the field was worth 20,000 men to his side. He was of noble character, a simple, straightforward soldier, devout and God-fearing, a true patriot, prepared to give his life for his country, great in every situation, under every condition, unspoilt by success, unshaken by adversity. "A large austere man," Ulysses Grant called him, and he was no doubt clothed with a natural dignity that was most impressive; but he had still a keen sense of humour, and ruled by quiet sarcasm as much as by force and severity. One good story is told of his rebuke to Mr. Hill, the newspaper editor who freely found fault with one of his campaigns:

> We made a great mistake, Mr. Hill, at the beginning of the war, and that was in appointing our best generals to edit newspapers and our worst to command the armies in the field. For myself, I have done my best, but I shall be happy to change places with you if you can do better.

Another story shows him in the finest light, his large-minded chivalry and unstinting kindliness of heart. It was after this very Battle of Gettysburg about to be described, at which he was defeated, as we shall see. When he had ordered a general retreat and was passing rapidly to the rear, he came close to where a wounded Union soldier lay upon the ground with a shattered leg. The poor fellow, with a fine bravado that no one can condemn, raised himself up at recognising the enemy's general and shouted "Hurrah for the Union!" full in Lee's face. Then Lee—but let the veteran tell his own story:

> The general heard me, looked, stopped his horse, dismounted and came towards me. I confess that I at first thought he meant to kill me. But as he came up he looked down at me with such a sad expression on his face that all fear left me and I wondered what he was about. He extended his hand to me, and grasping mine firmly and looking right into my eyes he said, 'My son, I hope you will soon be well.' If I live a thousand years I shall never forget the expression on General Lee's face. There he was, defeated, retiring from a field that had cost him and his cause almost their last hope, and yet he stopped to say words like these to a wounded soldier of the opposition, who had taunted him as he passed by. As soon as the general had left me I cried myself to sleep, there upon the bloody ground.

No wonder that "Mas'r Robert," as he was affectionately called in the army and throughout the South, was the idol of his men. Whenever he showed himself he was greeted with that fierce yell that came to be known as the Confederate battle-cry. When any at a distance heard it—if there was no fighting afoot, that is to say—they knew its meaning, and would exclaim, "There goes Mas'r Robert, or old Stonewall Jackson, or a hunted hare." His anxiety for his men was unbounded; his first care was for the sick and wounded. When his grateful fellow countrymen would have presented him with a house and estate, he refused, begging that the money might be distributed among the sufferers in the war. He chided his officers when they exposed themselves needlessly, and if they retorted that they only followed his example, he would say that it was his duty to be in the forefront and not theirs. Yet sometimes his people protested when his ardent courage carried him too far. In one of the fierce encounters in the Wilderness he rode up, resolved to lead the charge. Then the officer commanding cried, "General Lee, this is no place for you. Boys! is it necessary for General Lee to show you the way?"

"No! No!" was the ringing reply. "We will drive the enemy back if General Lee will only go to the rear."

It is sad to turn from this splendid old man in his triumphs to the hour when he was forced to surrender the remnant of his gallant band to General Grant. Even then the affection of those he had so often led to victory was exhibited in the most touching fashion. They would have cheered him as he rode by on that same grand war-horse. Traveller, who had carried him almost uninterruptedly through the war, but the sadness of the occasion silenced all. Only as he rode slowly along the lines hundreds of his devoted veterans pressed around their noble chief, trying to take his hand, touch his person, or even lay a hand upon his horse, thus exhibiting their great affection for him. The general then, with head bare and tears flowing down his manly checks, bade *adieu* to the army. In a few words he told the brave men who had been so true in arms to return to their homes and become worthy citizens.

It was in June, 1863, when Lee was at the zenith of his reputation, that he resolved to follow up the successes already achieved against the North by an invasion of the Northern territory. The strategical operations he now adopted, and which led up to his reverse at Gettysburg, must be described here with a view to a proper appreciation of the coming battle.

At this time the Confederate forces in Virginia numbered 70,000. Opposed to them were about 80,000 Federals under General "Joe" Hooker, a comparatively weak force owing, as has been said, to the action of the Short Service EnlistmentAct, under which many had recently left the colours. Besides these 40,000 more were in and about Washington under *quasi*-independent commanders, following the vicious system that then obtained, and none were available for the first line. Hooker's army, covering Washington, was encamped on the Rappahannock River immediately opposite the lines of Fredericksburg, which were at this time held by the bulk of the Confederate Army.

Lee was anxious to take the offensive, both to draw Hooker away and to transfer the theatre of war to beyond the Potomac. With these objects he began on the 3rd of June a rapid concentration to his left. First Longstreet's corps, then Ewell's were directed upon Culpepper Court House, while Hill stood fast at Fredericksburg watching Hooker. The latter was long in ignorance of his enemy's movements, but on the 9th June he learnt through a cavalry skirmish that Lee was in force at Culpepper. Hooker meant to follow along the river, but now Lee made a further bold leap ahead and stretched out Ewell's corps north and west, thus thrusting his extreme left into the valley of the Shenandoah. Ewell was at Winchester on the 13th, having accomplished seventy miles from Culpepper in three days. Lee's front now occupied at least a hundred miles. His right corps, Hill's, was still at Fredericksburg; Longstreet with the centre was at Culpepper; the left and most advanced was at Winchester at the mouth of the Shenandoah Valley, still remembered by the Federals, from the many disasters encountered there, as the "Valley of Humiliation."

Hooker, when he realised that Lee was thus dangerously drawn out, was for striking at once against his centre, but he was not encouraged therein by the Government in Washington, and he had no alternative but to retire and cover the capital. This released the Confederate General Hill from Fredericksburg, and he quickly followed on to Culpepper, thus relieving Longstreet, who now marched northward, taking the eastern slope of the Blue Ridge mountain, and pointing for Harper's Ferry on the Potomac. Hill then slipped in behind and threaded the Shenandoah Valley in support of Ewell. Ewell, knowing the others were approaching, now pushed across the Potomac and invaded Pennsylvania. Longstreet and Hill followed Ewell, and then the whole of this Northern territory was at the mercy of the Confederate

Army.

At this critical moment when grave events were imminent, General Hooker fell out with his superiors and resigned his command. His conduct has been sharply criticised, but he no doubt felt that he was not a free agent, and had been subjected to too much fussy interference. He was immediately replaced by General Meade, a much more practical soldier, who had made his way upward by sterling merit, who was quiet and undemonstrative but strong and self-reliant, knowing his business thoroughly. The President—Lincoln— appears to have trusted in him implicitly, and he was at once given fuller powers than Hooker had enjoyed.

Meade felt that it was incumbent upon him to come to blows with Lee as soon as possible. He guessed the enemy's intentions from the direction of his march, and hoped that by striking promptly at Lee he might turn him back and prevent him from crossing the Susquehanna River.

The Federal Army had been converging on Frederick City, and had already reached it when Meade assumed the command. From Frederick he at once moved forward towards Gettysburg.

Meade had seven army corps under his orders. The first (Reynolds) and eleventh (Howard) were directed on Emmetsburg; the third (Sickles) and the twelfth (Slocum) on Taneytown; the second (Hancock) on Frizzleburg; the fifth (Sykes) to Unionville, and the sixth corps (Sedgwick) to Windsor.

This was the 29th June. On that same day General Lee learnt that the Federals were on the move, and with a celerity which they had never before displayed. Fearing for his now greatly extended communications, he desisted from his plan of invasion, and resolved to concentrate rapidly so as to be ready, if necessary, to cover his line of retreat. Accordingly, he at once countermarched Ewell from York back on Gettysburg, and diverted Longstreet and Hill from Chambersburg to the eastward, also on Gettysburg. The opposing armies were thus rapidly approaching each other; a great battle was evidently near at hand, although no one as yet could surely forecast the exact spot on which it would take place.

Lee was pointing for Gettysburg because it was of supreme importance to him. Meade, who had no such strong reason, was also making for it: he had at that time no knowledge of the lie of the land there and the strong features it offered as a position to defend, but he merely threw his advance forward to seize and occupy it as a cover for a general line he meant to assume along Pipe Creek. This advanced force consisted of three army corps—the 1st, 3rd. and 11th, the whole under the command of General Reynolds of the 1st Corps. The march of this force was preceded by a division of cavalry, Buford's.

Buford seized Gettysburg on the 30th June, and pushing through it reconnoitred west and north by roads along which Lee was expected. That night Lee's advance, two divisions of Hill's corps, having threaded the passes of the South Mountain, bivouacked within seven miles of Gettysburg; the head of Ewell's corps was at Heidelsburg, nine miles; Longstreet's corps and Hill's third division were still to the westward of South Mountain. General Lee with headquarters was with Longstreet.

THE FIRST DAY'S BATTLE.

On the morning of the 1st June, Buford with the Federal cavalry stood across to Chambersburg, and was attacked by Hill about 9 a.m. Buford made good dispositions, resolving to hold the Confederates in check until he could be supported: he knew that Reynolds with two whole army corps was not far off, and that it was his duty to detain the enemy as long as possible. Reynolds hurried everyone forward, and soon became hotly engaged with the 1st Corps, which was the earliest and only one to reach the ground for some time. Reynolds had no orders to bring on a general action, but he knew that the bulk of his friends were still to the rear, and he was anxious to give them time to come up and form in the position south of Gettysburg.

The first fight was on either side of the Chambersburg road, especially to the south along a small river called Willoughby's Run, and here while nobly animating his men Reynolds was slain. Next Ewell's corps, arriving from the northward, began to exert pressure on the Federal right, and a portion of the 1st Corps was moved across to meet it; presently the arrival of the 11th Corps under Howard brought further help. Howard was now the senior officer and in chief command. He fell into an error not uncommon during this war—that of attempting to cover too much ground. The result was that the long Federal line was unduly weak and drawn out with dangerous gaps at critical points.

One of these was about Oak Hill, a commanding ridge between the right of the 1st Corps and the left of the 11th. Rodes, with the advance division of Ewell's corps reaching towards his right to join hands with Hill, saw this opening and seized it, thus securing the key-point of the Federal position. While Ewell's other division under Early easily forced back, the extreme right, Rodes, thus happily placed, broke through the centre with irresistible force, and the whole of the Federal line was broken, its several component parts retreating in great disorder towards the town of Gettysburg. So serious was the reverse that the Confederates captured 5,000 prisoners, and as many more Federal soldiers were left dead or wounded on the ground.

Meanwhile Meade had hurriedly sent General Hancock forward to assume the command and use his discretion as to the position the whole army should assume, whether it should hold Gettysburg or occupy the proposed line of Pipe Creek. Hancock's first duty, however, was to rally the disorganised 1st and 11th Corps, and, being a calm, self-reliant man whose soldierly qualities were well known to the troops, he soon restored order and established the shaken forces firmly in the new and strong position he found ready to his hand. For Hancock, with true military perception, had taken in at a glance the value of the ground just south of Gettysburg for defensive purposes. He accordingly urged the general-in-chief to occupy it at once and make it his battleground. Meade readily concurred, and moved up all the troops he had in hand to support those already in position there.

This ridge of Gettysburg—a name that will be ever famous in military history—is no doubt admirably adapted for defence. It runs due south of the town, but at a point opposite it and near it the ridge trends back to the east, thus forming a salient angle or "crotchet." The centre is known as Cemetery Hill. To the right and east is another higher hill. Culp's Hill, which is rough and rocky, its base washed by a stream. This hill formed the extreme right of the Federal position. South from Cemetery Hill the ridge runs strongly defined for three miles, then ends in two high peaks, rocky and wooded, the most elevated being known as "Round Top," the lesser as "Little Round Top" Hills. The eastern slope of the position was good but gradual, affording excellent cover for reserves and trains. The western front sloped more steeply down to the valley, in which runs the Emmetsburg Road. On the far side is another ridge running parallel with Cemetery Ridge through part of its length; it is known as the Seminary Ridge, and was the centre of the Confederate position in the coming fights.

General Lee came upon the ground towards the close of the action which ended in the discomfiture of the two Federal Army corps. He was greatly hampered at this time for the want of cavalry, and much in the dark as to the enemy's exact movements or intentions.

The intrepid Stuart was his cavalry leader, but that famous general by an untoward manoeuvre had been quite cut off from him, and only rejoined by a wide detour on the 2nd July, his force much jaded and reduced by rapid marching. Lee, however, seems to have realised that a great battle was inevitable. He could see for himself that the Federals were collecting in front of him, and he hoped to be able to strike a blow before their concentration was complete.

Military critics have disapproved of Lee's decision to attack at this juncture. It is urged that the wiser strategy would. have been to draw off and make good his retreat before he was too gravely compromised at this great distance from his base. He was not now, indeed, very anxious to take the offensive unless his enemy gave him an advantage by some false move. But to have surrendered the invasion, to have re-crossed the Potomac without an action, would have been humiliating, for the Confederates were at this time in the ascendant. They had been so uniformly successful in late engagements that to retire now would have meant a terrible loss of prestige. Besides, they had always won hitherto: why not again? "There was not a barefoot soldier in tattered grey" among the Confederates who did not firmly believe then that Lee would certainly lead them to victory whenever he chose.

THE SECOND DAY'S BATTLE.

By the early morning of the 2nd July the opposing armies were gathered together around Gettysburg. All the Federal army corps, ex-cept Sedgwick's, had come up, and were thus disposed:—

1. Slocum with the 12th Corps held Culp's Hill on the extreme right.

2. Howard with the 11th Corps was posted at Cemetery Hill in the centre.

3. Hancock and the 2nd Corps came next along the southern ridge and then joined—

4. Sickles with the 3rd Corps on the left. The 5th Corps, under Sykes, was held in reserve at first behind the right, and later be-hind the left. On 1st July it was some twenty-three miles to the rear, but it came up after a rapid night march. Sedgwick and the 6th Corps was still further off—at Manchester, thirty-six miles distant, but he hurried forward, and covering the whole ground in twenty hours reached the field at 2 p.m. on this the 2nd July.

The Confederates were in positions as follow:

1. Ewell's corps occupied the town of Gettysburg and the ground in between it and Rock Creek. He held thus the left of Lee's line, and was opposed, naturally, to Culp's Hill, the Federal right.

2. Hill's corps was posted along the Seminary Ridge, which, as already described, fronted the Cemetery Ridge and centre of the Federal line.

3. Longstreet's corps had bivouacked four miles to the rear, but he was to circle round, take the right of the Confederates, and open the ball by an attack on the Federal left.

General Lee greatly hoped, as has been said, to commence the action before his opponents gathered up all their strength. An early reconnaissance made of the Cemetery Ridge encouraged this view, and decided him to throw his weight on the left of the enemy's line. He would have been all the more eager for this had he realised then what came out later—namely, that the two Round Top Hills on the Federal left were the keys of the position, and the Confederates, if lodged there, would have taken the whole length of the Cemetery Ridge in reverse. Longstreet, unfortunately, was too slow. That general could easily have covered the four miles that separated him from the battlefield in less than a couple of hours, but he waited and waited for one laggard brigade, a comparatively small body, until the day was nearly spent, and he did not commence his attack till 4 p.m. By this time the whole of the Federal forces had reached their ground.

Now when the hour of impact had arrived the Federal General Sickles gave the first chance to the Confederates. His post with the 3rd Corps was on the left extremity of the Cemetery Ridge, but short of the Round Top Hills. Seeing in front another crest some 500 yards distant and carrying the Emmetsburg road, he pushed forward and occupied it. He thus left a strong position for another, weaker, out of the line of the battle. This mistake was seized upon by Lee, who ordered Longstreet to make his first attack on Sickles's centre. It was done; while Hood, of Longstreet's corps, circled round, penetrated the right, and was within an ace of securing the Little Round Top. The crucial importance of this hill was very manifest to a Federal general of engineers, who was passing and who forthwith ordered up a brigade of Sykes's 5th Corps to hold it.

A race between Federals and Confederates for the Little Round Top followed, not unlike that of the English and French at Salamanca for the Arapiles Hills. The combatants joined issue and the prize was hotly contested steel to steel, but it was in the end retained by the blue-coated Federals and the battle saved. Meanwhile, Sickles was hardly pressed in the centre and had to be continually reinforced, first by Hancock's corps, and then by those of Sykes and Slocum, the last-named being brought up by Meade in person. In the end the Confederates gained the advanced ground taken up by Sickles, and it seemed a very substantial triumph. But this was not a part of the real position on Cemetery Ridge, and its importance was overestimated by Lee. A much greater gain had been achieved on the far right by Culp's Hill.

The plan of the Confederate battle had been to throw the chief burthen of attack upon Longstreet. But Ewell on the other, or extreme left, opposite the Federal right, was to make a vigorous demonstration against Culp's Hill so as to occupy the Federals on this side and keep back reinforcements from the threatened left. Ewell delayed his movement till near sunset, and thus failed in his object of retaining the whole of the 11th and 12th Corps in front of him.

But this told in his favour. So great had been the drain upon the Federal right to reinforce their endangered left that when Ewell advanced he boldly resolved to change demonstration into attack, and one of his divisions, Early's, all but captured Cemetery Hill. His second division, Johnson's, was sent up against Culp's Hill, where only a single brigade remained in position, and although it held out, bravely seconded by detachments from Wadsworth's division, the earthworks on Culp's Hill were carried and held by the Confederates all through that night. Their possession of this point jeopardised the whole Federal line, and rendered it practically untenable.

So at nightfall on this the second day's fighting, the advantage appeared to be with the Confederates. Longstreet had carried all before him, and Ewell was firmly established within the Federal line. There was much, therefore, to justify Lee in renewing the battle on the following day. Yet Meade was not disheartened. His losses had been terrible, already amounting to more than 20,000 men. But he was certain that his foes had also suffered most severely; he felt that his position, save at Culp's Hill, was intact, and he was strongly supported by the confidence with which his corps commanders declared that they could recover lost ground and hold their own the following day.

THE THIRD DAY'S BATTLE.

Lee had resolved to follow up his success at Culp's Hill, and to

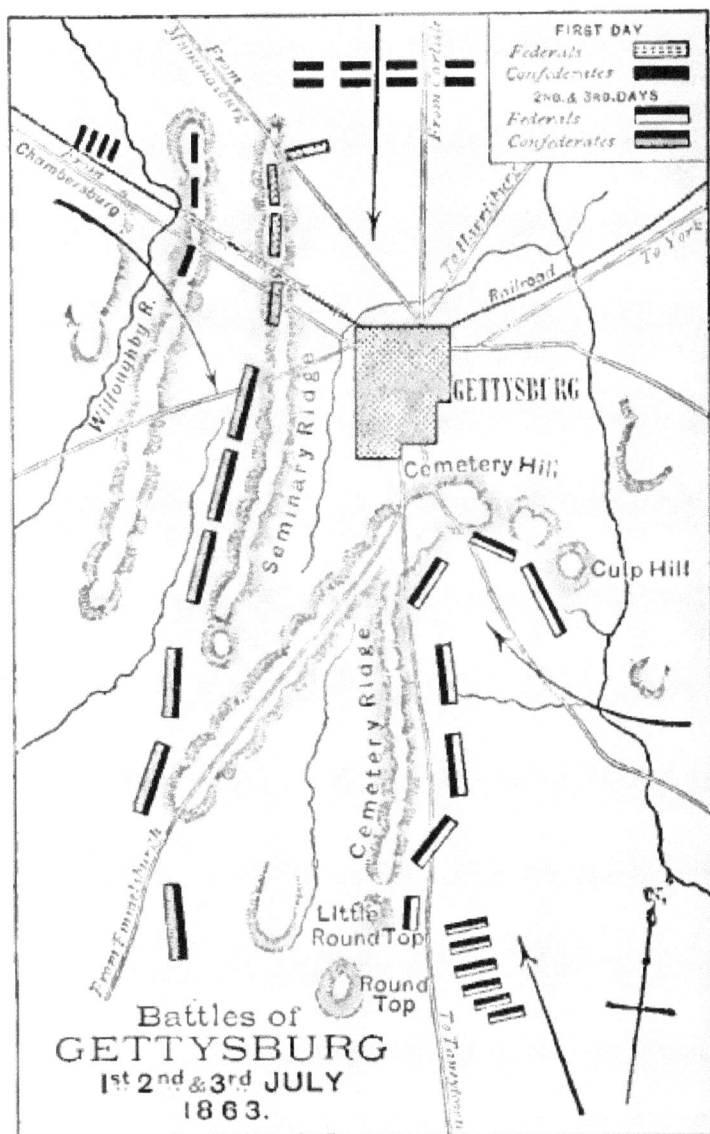

FIRST DAY
Federals
Confederates
2ND. & 3RD. DAYS
Federals
Confederates

From Mummasburg
From Carlisle
To Harrisburg
Chambersburg Rd.
To York
Railroad
Willoughby R.
Seminary Ridge
GETTYSBURG
Cemetery Hill
Culp Hill
Cemetery Ridge
From Emmettsburg
Little Round Top
Round Top
To Taneytown

Battles of
GETTYSBURG
1st 2nd & 3rd JULY
1863.

maintain at all costs and against all comers the foothold made by Johnson. But the Federal general was equally determined to turn him out, and during the night collected powerful field-batteries, which at daybreak opened a fierce fire upon the captured breastwork. Then two whole divisions of the 12th Corps and a fresh brigade of the 6th were sent by Meade to recover it. For four long hours the struggle went on until at last the hill was wrested from the Confederates, and the Federal line on this side was once more made secure.

Lee thereupon changed his plan and determined to attack the left centre of the Federal position at a point where the ridge was easier and the Emmetsburg road led through a depression. To prepare for this attack he massed his whole artillery on the Seminary Ridge, and by noon on the 3rd, 145 guns, all field-batteries, were in position. The Federals had not been idle meanwhile. They had gathered together eighty guns to reply to the enemy's cannonade, which commenced at 1 p.m., and is described by General Hancock as the most terrific he ever witnessed, "the most prolonged, one possibly hardly ever paralleled." This fearful artillery duel lasted for a couple of hours, when the fire of the Confederates gradually slackened as ammunition ran short, and that of the Federals was reserved to be directed with more crushing effect upon the attacking column.

The proud but perilous privilege of leading this attack was entrusted to Pickett's division of Longstreet's corps, which had only arrived upon the ground that morning, and was therefore fresh and not battle-torn. Pickett was to be supported by a division on the left (Pettigrew's) and a brigade (Wilcox's) on the right. It has since been declared that Lee intended Longstreet's two other divisions and a division of Hill's corps to take part in the attack, and it seems upon the face of it improbable that out of nine divisions Lee would have left two alone to carry out a momentous operation on which his fate and fortunes entirely depended. However, Pickett advanced 15,000 strong, crossing almost a mile of open "in such compact and imposing order that whether friend or foe, none who saw it could refrain from admiration of its magnificent array."

These splendid veterans of Virginia were soon shattered and decimated by such terrible artillery and musketry fire that the supporting columns paused abashed and left Pickett's men to attack single-handed. Undismayed, undeterred, they still pressed onward, and with one last heroic rush they crowned the heights, burst in upon the defenders, and were for a time victorious. But now the Federals, recovering,

THE SIGHT OF HIS FORM STIRRED THE HEARTS OF HIS VETERANS

rushed in on all sides, the fire of all the neighbouring guns was directed on Pickett's division, its right flank was assailed by a portion of a Vermont brigade. For some time, it maintained the unequal contest, but then the Confederates, "seeing themselves in a desperate strait, flung themselves on the ground to escape the hot fire, and threw up their hands in token of surrender, while the remnant sought safety in flight." Pettigrew's division had essayed to attack, but had been soon discomfited. Wilcox's brigade came on after Pickett's failure, but was soon driven back. Longstreet's divisions did not move.

The battle had now been lost and won. Whether or not the Federal general might have made his victory more complete by counterattack was much discussed at the time. The repulse of the Confederates might, it is thought, have been converted into absolute rout had Meade unleashed his legions and sent them out against the beaten Confederates. But his troops were mostly wearied; he had really no reserves in hand except the few fresh men belonging to Sedgwick's corps. Again, Lee and Longstreet both said afterwards they would have liked nothing better than to be attacked in their turn. Foreign officers with the Confederates state that it was well for the Federals that they did not attempt to follow up their advantage. Colonel (now General) Fremantle of our Brigade of Guards was also present, and, although he had grave fears of the consequences of a Federal attack, he describes the Confederates as but little broken by defeat.

> There was much less noise, fuss, or confusion of orders than at any ordinary field-day; the men as they were rallied in the woods were brought up in detachments, and lay down quietly and coolly in the positions assigned to them.

General Longstreet long afterwards gave it as his deliberate opinion that attack would have resulted disastrously.

> I had Hood's and McLaw's divisions, which had not been engaged; I had a heavy force of artillery; and I have no doubt I should have given those who tried as bad a reception as Pickett received.

General Meade was, however, a cautious commander. He knew that he had gained a great success, that Lee must now retreat, that the cause of the Confederacy had received a crushing blow from which it could never entirely recover. The cost, too, had been terrible: of Union soldiers no fewer than 23,000 were killed or disabled in the three days, and the losses inflicted on the Confederates rose still higher to 30,000. He was too well satisfied with the achievement to risk its results by any rash adventure.

So Lee was suffered to draw off, which he did that very night, retiring westward by passes through the South Mountain range into the Cumberland valley. Severe storms impeded his march, and the tail of his columns had not quite cleared from Gettysburg till the early morning of the 5th. Then Meade pursued, but still with great circumspection. When he came up with Lee about the 12th July, he found the Confederates in an entrenched position at Williamsport on the Potomac, designed to cover the passage of that river. There is a ford at this point, and Lee's engineers had improvised a pontoon bridge. Meade's forces were not fully collected till the 13th, and he had resolved to attack next morning. But at daylight on the 14th the Confederates had disappeared. Lee had withdrawn his last detachments during the night "with great skill and complete success."

They met, these doughty competitors, Lee and Meade, at the very end of the campaign, just after the Confederate surrender at Richmond. Meade, who was an old comrade in happier days before the fratricidal quarrel had set them in arms against each other, went to call in a friendly way upon Lee. In the course of a pleasant conversation Lee turned to his visitor and said, "Meade, the years are telling upon you: your hair is getting quite grey."

"Ah, General Lee," was Meade's rejoinder, "it is not the work of years: you are responsible for my grey hairs."

He was no doubt a dangerous antagonist. Critics have declared that, while Lee was peerless in defensive warfare, he was not so great in attack, and this judgment is perhaps borne out by the event at Gettysburg. But he attacked with great success at Chancellorsville, also at the second Battle of Manassas, and he was ready enough to strike a blow whenever he saw the opportunity. He too is taxed with being now over-cautious now over-bold. The truth was that he adapted himself to the occasion and employed strategy and tactics according to the character of the general opposed to him. He dared much with McClellan, Pope, and Hooker; with Grant he was patiently adroit and unweariedly tenacious.

In one respect he was unrivalled. No great soldier outvied him in the power of evoking the enthusiasm of his men. No privations, sufferings, disaster could shake their confidence in him. In the darkest hour the sight of his form or the mention of his name stirred the hearts of his veterans, and they spoke of him with affection and pride to his very last hour.

1

Gettysburg—Pickett's Charge

By James F. Crocker

AN ADDRESS BEFORE STONEWALL CAMP CONFEDERATE
VETERANS PORTSMOUTH: VIRGINIA NOVEMBER 7TH, 1894

You command me to renew an inexpressible sorrow, and to speak of those things of which we were a part

It is now nearly thirty years since there died away on the plains of Appomattox the sound of musketry and the roar of artillery. Then and there closed a struggle as heroic as ever was made by a brave and patriotic people for home government and home nationality. The tragic story of that great struggle has ever since been to me as a sealed, sacred book. I have never had the heart to open it. I knew that within its lids there were annals that surpassed the annals of all past times, in the intelligent, profound, and all-absorbing patriotism of our people—in the unselfish and untiring devotion of an entire population to a sacred cause—and in the brilliancy and prowess of arms which have shed an imperishable glory and honour on the people of this Southland. Yet there was such an ending to such great deeds!

The heart of this great people, broken with sorrow, has watered with its tears those brilliant annals until every page shows the signs of a nation's grief. And with it all there are buried memories as dear and as sacred as the ashes of loved ones. No, I have had no heart to open the pages of that sacred yet tragic history. Not until you assigned me the duty of saying something of Pickett's charge at the Battle of Gettysburg have I ever read the official or other accounts of that great battle; and when I lately read them my heart bled afresh, and my inward being was shaken to the deepest depths of sad, tearful emotions, and I wished that you had given to another the task you gave to me.

On the 13th day of December, 1862, Burnside lead his great and splendidly equipped army down from the heights of Fredericksburg, crossed the Rappahannock, and gave battle to Lee. His army was repulsed with great slaughter and was driven back bleeding and mangled to its place of safety. The star of Burnside went down and out. General Hooker was called to the command of the Army of the Potomac. After five months of recuperation and convalescence, with greatly augmented numbers and with every appliance that military art and national wealth could furnish in the perfect equipment of a great army, it was proclaimed with much flourish amidst elated hopes and expectancy, that his army was ready to move.

To meet this great host Lee could rely for success only on the great art of war and the unfailing courage of his soldiers. Hooker crossed the Rappahannock and commenced to entrench himself. Lee did not wait to be attacked, but at once delivered battle. The Battle of Chancellorsville was fought—the most interesting battle of the war—in which the blended genius of Lee and Jackson illustrated to the world the highest achievement of generalship in the management of the lesser against the greatly superior force. Again was the Army of the Potomac crushed and driven across the Rappahannock.

And now there arose a great question in the camp and in the council of State. It was a question of statesmanship as well as of arms. The question was answered by Lee withdrawing his army from before Hooker and proceeding through the lower Shenandoah Valley to Pennsylvania, leaving the road to Richmond open to be taken by the enemy if he should still prefer the policy of "on to Richmond." The motive of this movement was two-fold—to relieve Virginia of the enemy by forcing him to defend his own country, and by a possible great victory to affect public opinion of the North, and thus to conquer peace. The first object was accomplished; for as soon as Hooker discerned the movement of Lee, he hastened to follow and to put his army between Lee and Washington. Had Lee gained a crushing victory Baltimore and Washington would have been in his power, and then in all probability peace would have ensued. Public opinion in the North was greatly depressed, and sentiments of peace were ready to assert themselves. An incident illustrated this.

As we were marching from Chambersburg to Gettysburg, I observed some ladies near the roadway wave their handkerchiefs to our passing troops. It excited my attention and curiosity. I rode up to them and said, "Ladies, I observed you waving your handkerchiefs as if in cheer to our army. Why so? We are your enemies and the enemies of your country."

They replied: "We are tired of the war and want you to conquer peace."

I was greatly impressed with their answer, and saw that there might be true patriotism in their act and hopes.

The invasion of Pennsylvania was wise and prudent from the standpoint of both arms and statesmanship. Everything promised success. Never was the Army of Northern Virginia in better condition. The troops had unbounded confidence in themselves and in their leaders. They were full of the fervour of patriotism—had abiding faith in their cause and in the favouring will of Heaven There was an elation from the fact of invading the country of an enemy that had so cruelly invaded theirs. The spirit and *élan* of our soldiers was beyond description. They only could know it who felt it. They had the courage and dash to accomplish anything—everything but the impossible. On the contrary, the Federal Army was never so dispirited, as I afterwards learned from some of its officers. And this was most natural. They marched from the bloody fields of Fredericksburg and Chancellorsville, the scenes of their humiliating and bloody defeat, to meet a foe from whom they had never won a victory.

But alas, how different the result! Gettysburg was such a sad ending to such high and well assured hopes! Things went untoward with our generals. And Providence itself, on which we had so much relied, seems to have led us by our mishaps to our own destruction.

The disastrous result of the campaign, in my opinion, was not due to the generalship of Lee, but wholly to the disregard of his directions by some of his generals. The chief among these, I regret to say, was the failure of General Stuart to follow the order, (Lee's Report July 31, 1863, War Records, Series 1, Vol. 27, Part 2), of Lee, which directed him to move into Maryland, crossing the Potomac east or west of the Blue Ridge, as, in his judgment, should be best, and take *position on the right of our column as it advanced*. Instead of taking position on the right of our column as it advanced, Stuart followed the right of the Federal column, thus placing it between himself and Lee.

The consequence was that Lee from the time he crossed the Potomac had no communication with Stuart until after the battle on the 1st of July, when he heard that Stuart was at Carlisle, and Stuart did not reach Gettysburg until the afternoon of July 2nd. Lee, referring to Stuart, says:

> By the route he pursued the Federal Army was interposed between his command and our main body, preventing any communication with him until he arrived at Carlisle. The march toward Gettysburg was conducted more slowly than it would have been had the movements of the Federal Army been known.—War Records, Series 1, Vol. 27, Part 2.

These are solemn, mild words, but they cover the defeat at Gettysburg. Had Lee known the movements of the Federal army he could easily have had his whole army concentrated in Gettysburg on the 1st of July, and could easily have enveloped and crushed the enemy's advanced corps, and then defeated Meade in detail. But as it was, the encounter of the advance of the Federal Army was a surprise to Lee.

Hill had on the 30th of June encamped with two of his divisions, Heth's and Pender's at Cashtown, about eight miles from Gettysburg. Next morning, he moved with Heth's division, followed by Pender's toward Gettysburg. They encountered the enemy about three miles of the town. The enemy offered very determined resistance, but Heth's division, with great gallantry, drove him before it until it reached Seminary Heights, which overlooked Gettysburg.

At this time, 2 p. m., Rodes' and Early's divisions of Ewell's corps—the first from Carlisle and the other from York, made their opportune appearance on the left of Heth and at right angles to it; then Pender's division was thrown forward, and all advancing together drove the enemy from position to position, and through the town, capturing 5,000 prisoners, and putting the enemy to flight in great disorder. Referring to this juncture of affairs, Col. Walter H. Taylor, in his *Four Years with Genl. Lee*, says:

> Genl. Lee witnessed the flight of the Federals through Gettysburg and up the hills beyond. He then directed me to go to Genl. Ewell and to say to him that from the position he occupied he could see the enemy retiring over the hills, without organisation and in great confusion; that it was only necessary to press 'those people' in order to secure possession of the heights, and that, if possible, he wanted him to do this. In obedience to these instructions I proceeded immediately to Genl. Ewell and delivered the order of Genl. Lee.

Genl. Ewell did not obey this order. Those heights were what is known as Cemetery Hill, which was the key to the Federal position. The enemy afterward, that night, with great diligence fortified those heights; and subsequently the lives of thousands of our soldiers were sacrificed in the vain effort to capture them. It was a fatal disobedience of orders. What if Jackson had been there? Col. Taylor would not have had any order to bear to him. Lee would have witnessed not only the fleeing enemy, but at the same time the hot pursuit of Stonewall Jackson. Ah! if Stuart had been there, to give one bugle blast and to set his squadrons on the charge! Alas! he was then twenty-five miles away at Carlisle, ignorant that a battle was on.

That afternoon after the fight was over, Anderson's division of Hill's corps arrived on the battlefield and took position where Pender formerly was. At sunset Johnson's division of Ewell's corps came up and took line of battle on Early's left, and about midnight McLaws' division and Hood's division (except Laws' brigade) of Longstreet's corps encamped within four miles of Gettysburg. The troops which had been engaged in the fight bivouacked on the positions won. I am thus particular to locate our troops in order to show who may be responsible for any errors of the next day.

Inasmuch as Meade's army was not fully up, it required no great generalship to determine that it would be to our advantage to make an attack as early in the next morning as possible. And it was no more than reasonable that every general having control of troops should feel and fully appreciate the imperious necessity of getting ready to do so and to be ready for prompt action.

General Lee determined to make the main attack on the enemy's left early in the morning. This attack was to be made by Longstreet, who was directed to take position on the right of Hill and on the Emmittsburg road. After a conference with the corps and division commanders the previous evening, it was understood that this attack was to be made as early as practicable by Longstreet, and he was to be supported by Anderson and to receive the co-operation of Ewell. General Fitzhugh Lee in his *Life of Lee*, says:

When Lee went to sleep that night he was convinced that his dispositions for the battle next day were understood by the corps commanders, for he had imparted them to each in person. On the morning of July 2, Lee was up before light, breakfasted and was ready for the fray.

Can you believe it? Can you even at this distant day altogether suppress a rising indignation—that Longstreet did not get into line of battle until after 4 p. m., although he had the previous night encamped within four miles of Gettysburg? In the meanwhile, Sickles had taken position in what is known as the Peach Orchard and on the Emmittsburg road, which were the positions assigned to Longstreet, and which he could have taken earlier in the day without firing a gun. The forces of the enemy had come up from long distances—Sedgwick had marched thirty-four miles since 9 p. m., of the day before and had gotten into line of battle before Longstreet did.

The attack was made. Sickles was driven from the Peach Orchard and the Emmittsburg road. Little Round Top and the Federal lines were penetrated, but they were so largely reinforced that the attack failed after the most courageous effort and great expenditure of lives. It has been stated that if this attack had been made in the morning as directed, Lee would have won a great victory, and the fighting of the 3rd would have been saved. The attack on the left also failed. There, too, the lines and entrenchments of the enemy were penetrated, but they could not be held for want of simultaneous and conjoint action on the part of the commanders. Col. Taylor, speaking of this, says: "The whole affair was disjointed."

Thus ended the second day. General Lee determined to renew the attack on the morrow. He ordered Longstreet to make the attack next morning with his whole corps, and sent to aid him in the attack of Heth's division under Pettigrew, Lane's and Scales' brigades of Pender's division under General Trimble, and also Wilcox's brigade, and directed General Ewell to assail the enemy's right at the same time. Lee says:

> A careful examination was made of the ground secured by Longstreet, and his batteries placed in position, which it was believed would enable them to silence those of the enemy. Hill's artillery and part of Ewell's was ordered to open simultaneously, and the assaulting column to advance under cover of the combined fire of the three. The batteries were directed to be pushed forward as the infantry progressed, protect their flanks and support their attacks closely.

Every word of this order was potentially significant. You will thus observe Lee's plan of attack. It was to be made in the morning—presumably in the early morning—with the whole of Longstreet's corps, composed of the divisions of Pickett, McLaws and Hood, together with Heth's division, two brigades of Pender and Wilcox's brigade,

THE CHARGE OF PICKETT, PETTIGREW, AND TRIMBLE, FROM A WAR-TIME SKETCH FROM THE UNION POSITION.

and that the assaulting column was to advance under the cover of the combined fire of the artillery of the three corps, and that the assault was to be the combined assault of infantry and artillery—the batteries to be pushed forward as the infantry progressed, to protect their flanks and support their attack closely. The attack was not made as here ordered. The attacking column did not move until 3 p. m., and when it did move it was without McLaws' and Hood's divisions and practically without Wilcox's brigade, and without accompanying artillery. The whole attacking force did not exceed 14,000, of which Pickett's division did not exceed 4,700. General Lee afterwards claimed that if the attack had been made as he ordered, it would have been successful.

In order to appreciate the charge made by the attacking force, it is necessary to have some idea of the relative strength and positions of the two armies, and of the topography of the country. Before the Battle of Gettysburg opened on the 1st of July, Meade's army consisted of seven army corps which, with artillery and' cavalry, numbered 105,000. Lee's army consisted of three army corps which, with artillery and cavalry, numbered 62,000. On the 3rd of July the enemy had six army corps in line of battle, with the Sixth corps held in reserve. Their right rested on Culp Hill and curved around westerly to Cemetery Hill, and thence extended southerly in a straight line along what is known as Cemetery Ridge to Round Top. This line was well protected along its whole length with either fortifications, stone walls or entrenchments. It was crowned with batteries, while the infantry was, in places, several ranks deep, with a line in the rear with skirmish lines in front.

The form of the line was like a shepherd's crook. Our line extended from the enemy's right to Seminary Ridge, which runs parallel to Cemetery Ridge, to a point opposite to Round Top. Between these two ridges lay an open, cultivated valley of about one mile wide, and through this valley ran the Emmittsburg road in a somewhat diagonal line, with a heavy fence on either side. The charge was to be made across this valley so as to strike the left centre of the enemy's line. The hope was that if we broke their line, we would swing around to the left, rout and cut off their right wing, where Stuart waited with his cavalry to charge upon them; and thus destroy or capture them, and put ourselves in possession of the Baltimore road and of a commanding position.

Such were the plans of the assault and such was the position of the hostile forces. Lee's plan to make an assault was dangerous and hazardous, but he was pressed by the force of circumstances which we cannot now consider. The success of his plan depended largely on the promptness and co-operation of his generals. Without this there could be little hope of success. He gave his orders and retired for tomorrow.

All wait on the tomorrow. And now the 3rd of July has come. The summer sun early heralded by roseate dawn, rises serenely and brightly from beyond the wooded hills. No darkening clouds obscure his bright and onward way. His aspect is as joyous as when Eden first bloomed under his rays. Earth and heaven are in happy accord. The song of birds, the chirp and motion of winged insects greet the early morn. The wild flowers and the cultivated grain of the fields are glad in their beauty and fruitage. The streams joyously ripple on their accustomed way, and the trees lift and wave their leafy branches in the warm, life-giving air. Never was sky or earth more serene—more harmonious—more aglow with light and life.

In blurring discord with it all was man alone. Thousands and tens of thousands of men—once happy fellow countrymen, now in arms, had gathered in hostile hosts and in hostile confronting lines. It was not the roseate dawn nor rising sun that awoke them from the sleep of wearied limbs. Before the watching stars had withdrawn from their sentinel posts, the long roll, the prelude of battle, had sounded their reveille, and rudely awoke them from fond dreams of home and loved ones far away. For two days had battle raged. On the first, when the field was open and equal, the soldiers of the South, after most determined resistance, had driven their foe before them from position to position—from valley to hill top, through field and through the town, to the heights beyond.

On the second day, on our right and on our left, with heroic valour and costly blood, they had penetrated the lines and fortifications of the enemy, but were too weak to hold the prize of positions gained against overpowering numbers of concentrated reinforcements. The dead and wounded marked the lines of the fierce combat. The exploded caissons, the dismounted cannon, the dead artillery horses, the scattered rifles, the earth soaked with human gore—the contorted forms of wounded men, and the white, cold faces of the dead, made a mockery and sad contrast to the serene and smiling face of the skies.

From the teamsters to the general in chief it was known that the battle was yet undecided—that the fierce combat was to be renewed. All knew that victory won or defeat suffered, was to be at a fearful cost—that the best blood of the land was to flow copiously as a priceless oblation to the god of battle. The intelligent soldiers of the South knew and profoundly felt that the hours were potential—that on them possibly hung the success of their cause—the peace and independence of the Confederacy. They knew that victory meant so much more to them than to the enemy. It meant to us uninvaded and peaceful homes under our own rule and under our own nationality. With us it was only to be let alone.

With this end in view, all felt that victory was to be won at any cost. All were willing to die, if only their country could thereby triumph. And fatal defeat meant much to the enemy. It meant divided empire—lost territory and severed population. Both sides felt that the hours were big with the fate of empire. The sense of the importance of the issue, and the responsibility of fully doing duty equal to the grand occasion, impressed on us all a deep solemnity and a seriousness of thought that left no play for gay moods or for sympathy with nature's smiling aspect, however gracious. Nor did we lightly consider the perils of our duty. From our position in line of battle, which we had taken early in the morning, we could see the frowning and cannon-crowned heights far off held by the enemy.

In a group of officers, a number of whom did not survive that fatal day, I could not help expressing that it was to be another Malvern Hill, another costly day to Virginia and to Virginians. While all fully saw and appreciated the cost and the fearful magnitude of the assault, yet all were firmly resolved, if possible, to pluck victory from the very jaws of death itself. Never were men more conscious of the difficulty imposed on them by duty, or more determinedly resolved to perform it with alacrity and cheerfulness, even to annihilation, than were the men of Pickett's division on that day. With undisturbed fortitude and even with ardent impatience did they await the command for the assault. The quiet of the day had been unbroken save on our extreme left, where in the early morning there had been some severe fighting; but this was soon over, and now all on both sides were at rest, waiting in full expectancy of the great assault, which the enemy, as well as we, knew was to be delivered.

The hours commenced to go wearily by. The tension on our troops had become great. The midday sun had reached the zenith, and poured its equal and impartial rays between the opposite ridges that bounded the intervening valley running North and South. Yet no sound or stir broke the ominous silence. Both armies were waiting spectators for the great event. Upwards of one hundred thousand unengaged soldiers were waiting as from a grand amphitheatre to witness the most magnificent heroic endeavour in arms that ever immortalized man. Still the hours lingered on. Why the delay? There is a serious difference of opinion between the general in chief and his most trusted lieutenant general as to the wisdom of making the assault.

Lee felt, from various considerations, the forced necessity of fighting out the battle here, and having the utmost confidence in his troops he fully expected victory if the attack be made as he had ordered. Longstreet, foreseeing the great loss of assaulting the entrenched position of the enemy and making such assault over such a distance under the concentrated fire, urges that the army should be moved beyond the enemy's left flank, with the hope of forcing him thus to abandon his stronghold or to fight us to our advantage. Longstreet pressed this view and delayed giving the necessary orders until Lee more peremptorily repeated his own order to make the assault. Even then Longstreet was so reluctant to carry out the orders of Lee that he placed upon Lt.-Col. Alexander, who was in charge of the artillery on this day, the responsibility of virtually giving the order for its execution.

At last, in our immediate front, at 1 p. m., there suddenly leaped from one of our cannons a single sharp, far-reaching sound, breaking the long-continued silence and echoing along the extended lines of battle and far beyond the far-off heights. All were now at a strained attention. Then quickly followed another gun. Friend and foe at once recognized that these were signal guns. Then hundreds of cannon opened upon each other from the confronting heights. What a roar—how incessant! The earth trembled under the mighty resound of cannon. The air is darkened with sulphurous clouds. The whole valley is enveloped. The sun, lately so glaring, is itself obscured.

Nothing can be seen but the flashing light leaping from the cannon's mouth amidst the surrounding smoke. The air which was so silent and serene is now full of exploding and screaming shells and shot, as if the earth had opened and let out the very furies of Avernus. The hurtling and death-dealing missiles are ploughing amidst batteries, artillery and lines of infantry, crushing, mangling and killing until the groans of the men mingle with the tempest's sound. The storm of battle rages. It is appalling, terrific, yet grandly exciting. It recalls the imagery of Byron's night-storm amidst the Alps:

The sky is changed, and such a change!
Far along

From peak to peak, the rattling crags among
Leaps the live thunder! Not from one lone cloud,
But every mountain now hath found a tongue,
And Jura answers from her misty shroud
Back to the joyous Alps who call to her aloud.

After two hours of incessant firing the storm at last subsides. It has been a grand and fit prelude to what is now to follow. All is again silent. Well knowing what is shortly to follow, all watch in strained expectancy. The waiting is short. Only time for Pickett to report to his lieutenant-general his readiness and to receive the word of command.

Pickett said: "General, shall I advance?"

Longstreet turned away his face and did not speak. Pickett repeated the question. Longstreet, without opening his lips, bowed in answer.

Pickett, in a determined voice, said: "Sir, I shall lead my division forward," and galloped back and gave the order, "Forward march!"

The order ran down through brigade, regimental and company officers to the men. The men with alacrity and cheerfulness fell into line. Kemper's brigade on the right, Garnett's on his left, with Heth's division on the left of Garnett, formed the first line. Armistead's brigade moved in rear of Garnett's, and Lane's and Scales' brigades of Pender's division moved in the rear of Heth, but not in touch nor in line with Armistead. As the lines cleared the woods that skirted the brow of the ridge and passed through our batteries, with their flags proudly held aloft, waving in the air, with polished muskets and swords gleaming and flashing in the sunlight, they presented an inexpressibly grand and inspiring sight.

It is said that when our troops were first seen there ran along the line of the Federals, as from men who had waited long in expectancy, the cry: There they come! There they come! The first impression made by the magnificent array of our lines as they moved forward, was to inspire the involuntary admiration of the enemy. Then they realized that they came, terrible as an army with banners. Our men moved with quick step as calmly and orderly as if they were on parade.

No sooner than our lines came in full view, the enemy's batteries in front, on the right and on the left, from Cemetery Hill to Round Top, opened on them with a concentrated, accurate and fearful fire of shell and solid shot. These ploughed through or exploded in our ranks, making great havoc. Yet they made no disturbance. As to the orderly conduct and steady march of our men, they were as if they had not been. As the killed and wounded dropped out, our lines closed and dressed up, as if nothing had happened, and went on with steady march. I remember I saw a shell explode amidst the ranks of the left company of the regiment on our right. Men fell like ten-pins in a ten-strike.

Without a pause and without losing step, the survivors dressed themselves to their line and our regiment to the diminished regiment, and all went on as serenely and as unfalteringly as before. My God! it was magnificent—this march of our men. What was the inspiration that gave them this stout courage—this gallant bearing—this fearlessness—this steadiness—this collective and individual heroism? It was home and country. It was the fervour of patriotism—the high sense of individual duty. It was blood and pride of state—the inherited quality of a brave and honourable ancestry.

On they go—down the sloping sides of the ridge—across the valley—over the double fences—up the slope that rises to the heights crowned with stone walls and entrenchments, studded with batteries, and defended by multiple lines of protected infantry. The skirmish line is driven in. And now there bursts upon our ranks in front and on flank, like sheeted hail, a new storm of missiles—canister, shrapnel and rifle shot. Still the column advances steadily and onward, without pause or confusion. Well might Count de Paris describe it as an irresistible machine moving forward which nothing could stop. The dead and wounded—officers and men—mark each step of advance.

Yet under the pitiless rain of missiles the brave men move on, and then with a rush and cheering yell they reach the stone wall. Our flags are planted on the defences. Victory seems within grasp, but more is to be done. Brave Armistead, coming up, overleaps the wall and calls on all to follow. Brave men follow his lead. Armistead is now among the abandoned cannon, making ready to turn them against their former friends. Our men are widening the breach of the penetrated and broken lines of the Federals. But, now the enemy has made a stand, and are rallying. It is a critical moment. That side must win which can command instant reinforcements. They come not to Armistead, but they come to Webb, and they come to him from every side in overwhelming numbers in our front and with enclosing lines on either flank. They are pushed forward.

Armistead is shot down with mortal wounds and heavy slaughter is made of those around him. The final moment has come when there must be instant flight, instant surrender, or instant death. Each alternative is shared. Less than 1,000 escape of all that noble division which in the morning numbered 4,700; all the rest either killed, wounded or captured. All is over. As far as possible for mortals they approached the accomplishment of the impossible. Their great feat of arms has closed. The charge of Pickett's division has been proudly, gallantly and right royally delivered.

And then, at once, before our dead are counted, there arose from that bloody immortalised field, Fame, the Mystic Goddess, and from her trumpet in clarion notes there rang out upon the ear of the world the story of Pickett's charge at Gettysburg. All over this country, equally North and South, millions listened and returned applause. Over ocean Fame wing's her way. Along the crowded population and cities of Europe she rings out the story. The people of every brave race intently listen and are thrilled. Over the famous battlefields of modern and ancient times she sweeps. Over the ruins and dust of Rome the story is heralded. Thermopylae hears and applauds.

The ancient pyramids catch the sound, and summing up the records of their hoary centuries, searching, find therein no story of equal courage. Away over the mounds of buried cities Fame challenges, in vain, a response from their past. Over the continents and the isles of the sea the story runs. The whole world is tumultuous with applause. A new generation has heard the story with undiminished admiration and praise. It is making its way up through the opening years to the opening centuries. The posterities of all the living will gladly hear and treasure it, and will hand it down to the end of time as an inspiration and example of courage to all who shall hereafter take up arms.

The intrinsic merit of the charge of Pickett's men at Gettysburg, is too great, too broad, too immortal for the limitations of sections, of states, or of local pride.

The people of this great and growing republic, now so happily reunited, have and feel a common kinship and a common heritage in this peerless example of American courage and American heroism.

But let us return to the battlefield to view our dead, our dying and our wounded. Here they lie scattered over the line of their march; here at the stone wall they lie in solid heaps along its foot; and here within the Federal lines they are as autumnal leaves—each and all precious heroes—each the loved one of some home in dear, dear Virginia. Now we seem to catch the sound of another strain. It is more human; it touches pathetically more closely human hearts. It is the wailing voice of afflicted love. It is the sobbing outburst of the sorrow of bereavement coming up from so many homes and families, from so many kinsmen and friends; and with it conies the mournful lamentations of Virginia herself, the mother of us all, over the loss of so many of her bravest and best sons.

Of her generals Garnett is dead, Armistead is dying; and Kemper desperately wounded. Of her colonels of regiments six are killed on the field, Hodges, Edmonds, Magruder, Williams, Patton, Allen, and Owen is dying and Stuart mortally wounded. Three lieutenant-colonels are killed, Calcutt, Wade and Ellis. Five colonels, Hunton, Terry, Garnett, Mayo and Aylett, are wounded. Four lieutenant-colonels commanding regiments, Martin, Carrington, Otey and Richardson are wounded. Of the whole complement of field officers in fifteen regiments only one escaped unhurt, Lieutenant-Colonel Joseph C. Cabell. The loss of company officers are in equal proportion. It is a sad, mournful summing up. Let the curtain fall on the tragic scene.

But there are some of those who fell on that field whom I cannot pass by with a mere enumeration.

Gen. Lewis A. Armistead, the commander of our brigade, is one of these. Fortune made him the most advanced and conspicuous hero of that great charge. He was to us the very embodiment of a heroic commander. On this memorable day he placed himself on foot in front of his brigade. He drew his sword, placed his hat on its point, proudly held it up as a standard, and strode in front of his men, calm, self-collected, resolute and fearless. All he asked was that his men should follow him. Thus in front he marched until within about one hundred paces of the stone wall some officer on horseback, whose name I have never been able to learn, stopped him for some purpose. The few moments of detention thus caused were sufficient to put him for the first time in the rear of his advancing brigade. Then quickly on he came, and when he reached the stone wall where others stopped, he did not pause an instant—over it he went and called on all to follow. He fell, as above stated, amidst the enemy's guns, mortally wounded. He was taken to the Eleventh Corps' Hospital, and in a few days he died and was buried there.

Another: Col. James Gregory Hodges, of the 14th Virginia, of Armistead's brigade, fell instantly killed at the foot of the stone wall of the Bloody Angle, and around and over his dead body there was literally a pile of his dead officers around him, including gallant Major Poor. On the occasion of the reunion of Pickett's Division at Gettysburg,

1887, General Hunt, chief of the Federal artillery at this battle, who had known Col. Hodges before the war, pointed out to me where he saw him lying dead among his comrades. He led his regiment in this memorable charge with conspicuous courage and gallantry. He was an able and experienced officer. At the breaking out of the war he was Colonel of the Third Virginia Volunteers, and from 20th April, 1861, until he fell at Gettysburg he served with distinguished ability, zeal and gallantry his State and the Confederacy. He was with his regiment in every battle in which it was engaged in the war. He commanded the love and confidence of his men, and they cheerfully and fearlessly ever followed his lead. His memory deserves to be cherished and held in the highest esteem by his city, to which by his virtues, character and patriotic service he brought honour and consideration.

Col. John C. Owens, of the Ninth Virginia. Armistead's Brigade, also of this city, fell mortally wounded on the charge, and died in the field hospital that night. He had been recently promoted to the colonelency of the regiment from the captaincy of the Portsmouth Rifles, Company G. As adjutant of the regiment I had every opportunity of knowing and appreciating Col. Owens as a man and officer. I learned to esteem and love him. He was intelligent, quiet, gentle, kind and considerate. Yet he was firm of purpose and of strong will. He knew how to command and how to require obedience. He was faithful, and nothing could swerve him from duty.

Under his quiet, gentle manner there was a force of character surprising to those who did not know him well. And he was as brave and heroic as he was gentle and kind. Under fire he was cool, self-possessed, and without fear. He was greatly beloved and respected by his regiment, although he had commanded it for a very short time. He fell while gallantly leading his regiment before it reached the enemy's lines. He, too, is to be numbered among those heroes of our city, who left home, never to return; who after faithful and distinguished service, fell on the field of honour, worthy of the high rank he had attained, reflecting by his life, patriotism and courage, honour on his native city, which will never let his name and patriotic devotion be forgotten.

John C. Niemeyer, First Lieutenant I, Ninth Virginia, was killed in that charge just before reaching the famous stone wall. He was a born soldier, apt, brave, dashing. He was so young, so exuberant in feeling, so joyous in disposition, that in my recollection of him he seems to have been just a lad. Yet he knew and felt the responsibility of office, and faithfully and gallantly discharged its duties. He was a worthy brother of the distinguished Col. W. F. Niemeyer, a brilliant officer who also gave his young life to the cause.

And there, too, fell my intimate friend, John S. Jenkins, Adjutant of the Fourteenth Virginia. He, doubtless, was one of those gallant officers whom General Hunt saw when he recognised Colonel Hodges immediately after the battle, lying dead where he fell, who had gathered around him, and whose limbs were interlocked in death as their lives had been united in friendship and comradeship in the camp. He fell among the bravest, sealed his devotion to his country by his warm young blood, in the flush of early vigorous manhood when his life was full of hope and promise. He gave up home which was peculiarly dear and sweet to him, when he knew that hereafter his only home would be under the flag of his regiment, wherever it might lead, whether on the march, in the camp or on the battlefield. His life was beautiful and manly—his death was heroic and glorious, and his name is of the imperishable ones of Pickett's charge.

Time fails me to do more than mention among those from our city who were killed at Gettysburg: Lieut. Robert Guy, Lieut. George W. Mitchell, John A. F. Dundedale, Lemuel H. Williams, W. B. Bennett, John W. Lattimore, W. G. Monte, Richard J. Nash, Thomas C. Owens, Daniel Byrd, John Cross and Joshua Murden—heroes all—who contributed to the renown of Pickett's charge, gave new lustre to the prowess of arms, and laid a new chaplet of glory on the brow of Virginia, brighter and more immortal than all others worn by her.

Let marble shafts and sculptured urns
Their names record, their actions tell,
Let future ages read and learn
How well they fought, how nobly fell.

2

Gettysburg—Third Day
By LaSalle Corbell Pickett

Pickett's division—reserved for the last great scene in the tragedy of Gettysburg—had not yet entered the circle of fire which environed the mountains, filled the valleys with death, and turned the silvery streams into rivers of blood.

Until the night of July 1 the three brigades under Pickett's command, Corse and Jenkins having been left behind, remained on guard at Chambersburg. Being then relieved by Imboden, at two o'clock on the morning of the 2nd, they were under marching orders and moving along the Gettysburg road. In the pass of the South Mountain a fire flashed upon them from sharpshooters stationed in the gorges of the crags.

On the east side of the range the air trembled with the battle-rage of Gettysburg. The ardour of the men kindled into flame, and with eager, impatient feet they pressed forward to answer the call. Through the intense heat of one of the most fiery days with which July ever scorched the earth Pickett's men marched twenty-four miles and at two o'clock in the afternoon halted three miles from Gettysburg.

Though they were parched with heat and worn by the march, their commander sent his inspector-general. Colonel Walter Harrison, to report to Lee their position and condition and to tell him that, notwithstanding their fatigue, they could with two hours' rest be in any part of the field in which he might wish to use them.

Pickett rode on to meet Longstreet, who had expressed a desire to see him, and who, though relieved and delighted by his arrival upon the field, manifested great anxiety. While conversing with Longstreet Pickett viewed the ground and watched the fight in front of Little Round Top, where the other two divisions of Longstreet's corps under

George E. Pickett

Hood and McLaws, having started twenty-four hours in advance of his three brigades, had struck the corps commanded by Sickles. He was thus engaged when Colonel Harrison rode up with Lee's reply:

Tell General Pickett that I shall not want him this evening; to let his men rest, and I will send him word when I want him.

Pickett and Harrison left Longstreet still fighting with fearless tenacity in front of Round Top, and rode back to the division to seek such rest as they might find. They had viewed the field, had studied its advantages and disadvantages, had witnessed the terrific struggle, had watched A. P. Hill's attack upon the centre, thoroughly understood the situation, and knew that before them lay a dark and tragic day.

Lee had not been so successful on the second day as on the first, but he had gained some ground by a series of brilliant movements, and his repulses had been attended with heavy loss to the enemy. In his report he says:

These partial successes determined me to continue the assault next day.

On the afternoon of the 2nd Stuart came in from Carlisle and joined Lee on Seminary Ridge. He was followed by Kilpatrick, who lost about thirty men in a skirmish with Hampton, the latter having been left by Stuart at Hunterstown to prevent the Federal troopers from falling upon Ewell's rear.

Lee had concentrated more than a hundred guns against the left centre, under Hancock, posted on Cemetery Ridge, with Howard on the right and Sedgwick, Sykes, and Sickles on the left.

In the moonlight of that radiant night the Federals reformed their lines among their fallen comrades. Perhaps many a leader echoed in

HAND-TO-HAND FOR RICKETTS'S GUNS ON
THE EVENING OF THE SECOND DAY.
SEE P. 313.

43

STEUART'S BRIGADE RENEWING THE CONFEDERATE ATTACK ON CULP'S HILL, MORNING OF THE THIRD DAY.

his heart the softly breathed aspiration of Birney, "I wish I were already dead," as he looked upon the few who were left to follow him, and the many who lay in unbroken rest while the storm of battle swept unheeded over them.

As early as three o'clock on the morning of the 3rd of July Pickett's division was under arms and moving to the right and southeast of the Cashtown and Gettysburg road. Line of battle was formed, facing Cemetery Ridge, Kemper's brigade on the right, Garnett's on the left, and Armistead immediately in rear of Kemper and Garnett, there not being room for all in extended line of battle.

The fences and other obstructions were cleared away. The line was formed a little to the left of Meade's centre. On the left was Heth's division, commanded by Brigadier-General Pettigrew. To Pettigrew's left and rear were two brigades of Pender's division, commanded by Brigadier-General Trimble. Wilcox's brigade was lying about two hundred yards in front of our line. Orders were given to the men to lie down and keep still that they might not attract the attention of the enemy.

In obedience to a summons from Longstreet, Pickett rode to the top of the ridge in front, where Lee and Longstreet were making a reconnaissance of Meade's position, which seemed to be of invincible strength. The clouds of the early morning had drifted away and the sun shone out with intense brightness and heat. In its light were revealed all the difficulties of the ground between the Confederate line and the point of attack. Woods, streams, and steep hills impeded the movements of the Confederate guns and necessitated a fight with infantry against the Federal batteries. In the lower ground, beyond this space, the enemy had thrown out a very heavy skirmish-line. The ridge was defended by two tiers of artillery, supported by a double line of infantry. Heavy reserves of infantry were ranged in double column on the crest of the heights, protected by a stone wall extending along the side of the ridge. Across the lowland was a rail fence to obstruct the march of our troops. In order to come to close quarters with the enemy our men would be compelled to charge over half a mile of open ground in the face of a terrible rain of canister and shrapnel.

At twenty minutes to four the report of Geary's pistol rang out from the Federal lines, shivering the morning air with its ominous resonance. This was the signal for the beginning of the struggle for Culp's Hill, to which Geary's division had returned in the night. The contest was still in progress while Pickett stood with Lee and Long-

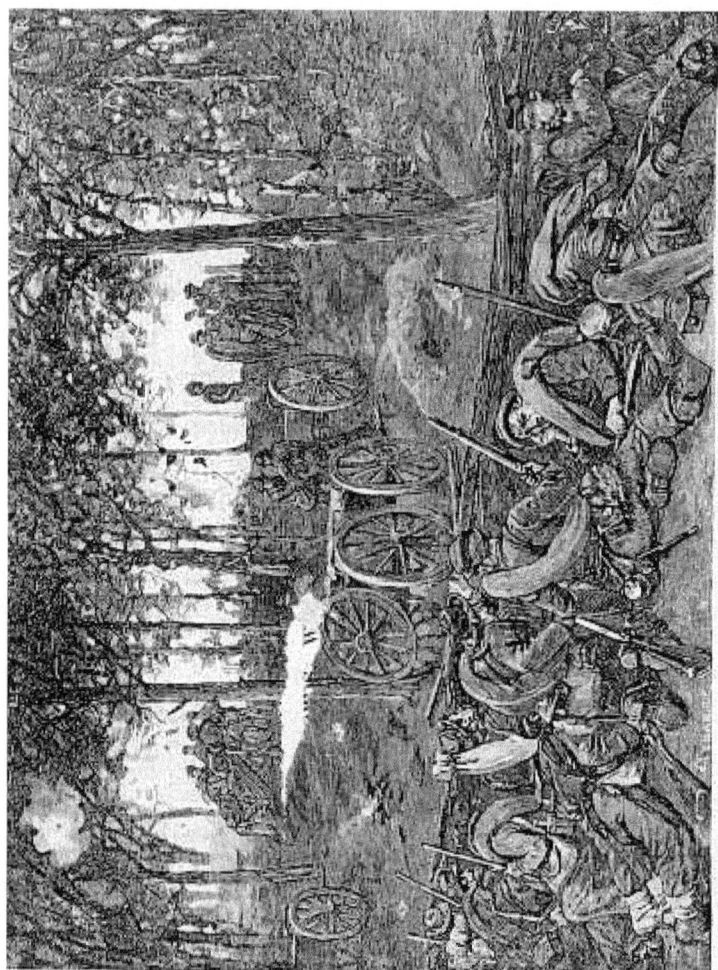

CONFEDERATES WAITING FOR THE END OF THE ARTILLERY DUEL.

street on the summit of the ridge. The Federal artillery on Power Hill and McAllister Hill swept the plateau on which Johnson was stationed and where he met the advancing infantry. He fought alone until eleven o'clock, when his battle was over and he fell back to Rock Creek.

About eight o'clock Pickett, in company with Lee and Longstreet, rode slowly up and down the long line of prostrate infantry, viewing them closely and critically. The men had been forbidden to cheer, but they voluntarily arose and stood silently with uncovered heads and hats held aloft, a motionless dark line against the white light of the morning with the gloom of the hills in the background. How many of those erect forms, standing so rigidly in soldierly strength and pride, would, when the sun should go down behind the purple hills, be lying on the plain beyond, nevermore to thrill with the ardour of earthly battles!

When this solemn, silent review was over detachments were thrown forward to support the artillery, consisting of one hundred and twenty cannon, stretched a mile along the crests of Oak Ridge and Seminary Ridge. For five hours the July sun poured its scorching rays almost vertically down upon the supporting detachments lying in the tall grass in the rear of the artillery-line, waiting in anxious suspense for some sound or movement to break the awful silence of the vast battlefield. The Federals on Cemetery Hill marvelled at the unexpected calm. Why did not the long-looked-for attack begin?

Anderson held the wood west of the wheat-field, a little to the north of Devil's Den. On the Emmitsburg road were six batteries of the First Corps, forming, with the rest of the artillery of this corps stationed near it, a slightly concave line of seventy-five pieces along the ridge which Humphreys had ineffectually tried to hold the day before. At the right of the orchard a cross-fire was effected by Henry's batteries. Alexander's were posted on the summit of a slope to the north, and on his left, a little to the rear, was the Washington Artillery, guarded by the battalions of Cabell and Dearing. Lee intended to batter the point of attack with Alexander's guns, which for that purpose were placed ahead of the infantry. The troops which were to make the attack were screened from view by the ridge, Pickett's three brigades being supported by one of Hill's light batteries. The assault was to be supported by Hill's artillery on Seminary Hill, and a part of Ewell's artillery was to fire on Cemetery Hill.

Signal-flags fluttered their portentous messages up and down the line—death-tokens alike to that living wall over which they waved and to the defenders of Cemetery Hill. The musketry and artillery fire, which opened at eleven o'clock, continued about three-quarters of an hour and then ceased.

Colonel J. J. Phillips, who had been with the division in every battle, relates the following to show how well the soldiers understood the work which had been marked out for them, and how far beyond their strength it was:

> A gallant son of old Isle of Wight County, before the charge was made, and while the artillery thundered over the plain, turned to me and said. 'We are ordered to charge those heights?' 'Yes,' said I. 'Then,' said he, 'this will be a sad day for Virginia.' After the battle another brave soldier. whose fame has compared the worlds said, 'This is a sad day for us.' He who said it before the battle was J. Frank Crocker, adjutant of the Ninth Virginia Infantry; and he who said it after the battle was General Robert E. Lee.

This reminiscence is recalled to show that Pickett's men marched into the very jaws of death with the full knowledge that they were offering up their lives on the altar of duty.

After the war. General Pickett said that he did not believe there was a man in his dear old division who did not know, when he heard the order, that in obeying it he was marching to death, yet every man of them marched forward unfalteringly.

It was one o'clock. The solemn silence which had reigned over the field was suddenly shivered.by a cannon-shot. A minute passed. The Washington Artillery again sent its ominous message thundering through the valley and echoing and re-echoing from the mountain-sides.

While the smoke from the gun still lingered over the plain, as if held down by the weight of its heavy meaning, and the echo was yet rolling along the distant defiles and gorges, the whole line was ablaze, and the thunder and crash of more than a hundred guns shook the hills from crest to base. From another hundred guns along the front of Cemetery. Ridge flashed forth an instant reply, and the greatest artillery duel of the western continent had begun.

The two ridges were about fourteen hundred yards apart, and were like great blazing volcanoes. A mighty roar as of all the thunderbolts of the universe filled the plain. No command could be heard through the shrieking shot and shell, for no sound of wind, water, volcano, thunder and cataract ever equalled this terrific uproar. The valley was filled with clouds of dust and suffocating smoke. A rolling sea of white and bluish and grey mist tossed its billows to and fro between the heights and blotted out the rays of the sun. The fierce flames from the guns flashed through, cutting the dark mists like lightning sabres in a Titanic battle of the clouds. Fiery fuses shot across the field, leaving death and mutilation in their murderous track. Flying missiles pierced the air, shells burst above troops, or tore up the ground and bounded off for another deadly strike. The Confederate line remained steady, although it was exposed to the fire of the enemy, which passed over the artillery and struck the infantry with terrible effect.

The ammunition was failing; the artillery combat must be closed. After two hours the firing ceased. For half an hour silence settled over the blackened field, during which time the Confederates were rapidly forming an attacking column just below the brow of Seminary Ridge. Long double lines of infantry came pouring out of the woods and levels, across ravines and little valleys, hurrying on to the positions assigned them in the column.

Two separate lines of double ranks were formed, a hundred yards apart, and in the centre of this column were the remnants of the three brigades of Pickett's division: Garnett's brigade, the Eighth, Eighteenth, Nineteenth, Twenty-Eighth and Fifty-Sixth Virginia; Armistead's brigade, the Ninth, Fourteenth, Thirty-Eighth, Fifty-Third and Fifty-Seventh Virginia; Kemper's brigade, First, Third, Seventh, Eleventh and Twenty-Fourth Virginia; numbering in all forty-seven hundred and sixty-one privates, two hundred and forty-four company officers, thirty-two field-officers and four general officers,

Pickett's three brigades were to attack in front where there was a bristling hedge of artillery and infantry. Heth's and Pender's divisions, under Pettigrew and Trimble, their leaders having been wounded the day before, were to charge in second and third lines of battle, supporting Pickett's advance. As Heth's division passed on it was to be joined by Wilcox's brigade, then about two hundred yards in front. Anderson was behind the two supporting divisions ready to take Trimble's place when he should leave it.

Pickett rode up to Longstreet for orders. The latter seemed greatly depressed and said:

> I do not want to have your men sacrificed, Pickett, so I have
> sent a note to Alexander, telling him to watch carefully the ef-

CONFEDERATE ARTILLERY AT DINNER.

fect of our fire upon the enemy, and that when it begins to tell he must take the responsibility and notify you himself when to make the attack. He has been directed to charge with you at the head of your line with a battery of nine eleven-pound howitzers, fresh horses and full caissons.

Just as Longstreet finished this statement a courier rode up and handed Pickett a note from Alexander, which read:

If you are coming, come at once or I cannot give you proper support, but the enemy's fire has not slackened at all. At least eighteen guns are still firing from the cemetery itself.

After Pickett had read the note he handed it to Longstreet.

"General Longstreet, shall I go forward?" he asked.

Longstreet looked at him with an expression which seldom comes to any face. In that solemn silence memories of the long friendship may have flooded his soul. Possibly there came to his thought the time away back in history when he had fallen on the stormy slope of Chapultepec, and the boy lieutenant had taken his place and borne the battle-flag in triumph to the flame-crowned height. He held out his hand and bowed his head in assent. Not a word did he speak.

"Then I shall lead my division forward, sir," said Pickett, and galloped off.

He had gone only a few yards when he came back and took a letter from his pocket. On it he wrote in pencil

If Old Peter's nod means death, goodbye, and God bless you, little one!

He gave the letter to Longstreet and rode back. That letter reached its destination in safety and, with its faint pencilled words, is now one of my most treasured possessions. It was transmitted with one from Longstreet:

Gettysburg. Penn., July 3rd

My Dear Lady: General Pickett has just intrusted to me the safe conveyance of the enclosed letter. If it should turn out to be his farewell the pencilled note on the outside will show you that I could not speak the words which would send so gallant a soldier into the jaws of a useless death. As I watched him, gallant and fearless as any knight of old, riding to certain doom, I said a prayer for his safety and made a vow to the Holy Father that my friendship for him, poor as it is, should be your heritage. We shall meet. I am, dear lady, with great respect.

Yours to command.

James Longstreet.

Pickett gave orders to his brigade commanders and rode along down the line, his men springing to their feet with a shout of delight as he told them what was expected of them.

He was sitting on his horse when Wilcox rode up. Taking a flask from his pocket, Wilcox said:

Pickett, take a drink with me. In an hour you'll be in hell or glory.

Pickett declined to drink, saying:

I promised the little girl who is waiting and praying for me down in Virginia that I would keep fresh upon my lips until we should meet again the breath of the violets she gave me when we parted. Whatever my fate. Wilcox. I shall try to do my duty like a man, and I hope that, by that little girl's prayers, I shall today reach either glory or glory.

At a quarter past three on that bright afternoon the order "Forward!" rang along the lines. The supreme moment had come. As far as the eye could reach, up and down on each side, the gaze of thousands of men of both armies was riveted on a long line of soldiers moving with all the precision of a grand review. The five thousand Virginians had begun their march to death.

Longstreet joined Alexander, and they stood together by the batteries when that magnificent column went by, the officers saluting as they passed.

Pickett led, mounted on his spirited charger, gallant and graceful as a knight of chivalry riding to a tournament. His long dark, auburn-tinted hair floated backward in the wind like a soft veil as he went on down the slope of death.

Then came Trimble, riding lightly as he might have ridden in the golden glow through the rose-scented air of some brilliant festal morning.

It was no holiday work to which they went as they gracefully saluted in passing their commanding general, who acknowledged it in silent sadness. "*Morituri, salutamus!*"

So they filed by, and went down into the heavy sea of smoke which

MAJOR-GENERAL CADMUS M. WILCOX, C. S. A.

MAJOR-GENERAL WILLIAM D. PENDER,
WOUNDED JULY 2, DIED JULY 18.

hid them from view. As it lifted they were seen moving in solid ranks with steady step and with the harmonious rhythm of some grand symphony. The sun caught the gleam of their guns and flashed it back in myriads of sparkling rays. Behind them was a wall of light against which their dark forms were outlined in distinct silhouette.

Pickett's Virginians were less than five thousand, but everyone was a soldier in the fullest sense of the word. As they pressed onward in majestic order over the plain, like a moving wall of granite, the battle-flag of the South waved over them, its stars shining as if in promise of victory.

Garnett was on the right; Armistead centre. Garnett had been ill for many days, traveling in the ambulance, but no persuasion could keep him from the post of danger. Too weak to mount his horse, he had insisted upon being placed in the saddle that he might lead his brigade in the charge.

The battle-smoke drifted away over the hills and into the clouds, where it arched itself above the field as if it would even yet spread a protecting mantle around those devoted men. The long Federal array with its double line of supports was revealed to view. As the advancing column came in sight Meade's guns opened upon it, but it neither paused nor faltered. Round shot, bounding along, tore through its ranks and ricocheted around it. Shells exploded, darting flashes before—behind—overhead.

A long line of skirmishers, prostrate on the grass, suddenly arose within fifty yards, firing at them as they came within view, then running on ahead, turning and firing back as fast as they could reload. The column took no heed of them, but moved on at a quickstep, not returning their fire.

Past the batteries and halfway over the field, amidst a terrific fire of shot and shell, Pickett gave the order, "Left oblique!" Coolly and beautifully the movement was made, changing the direction forty-five degrees from the front to the left.

From Cemetery Hill burst the fire of forty cannon against the right flank. Pickett's men fell like grain before the sweep of the scythe. There was no pause. The survivors pressed on with a force which seemed to have grown stronger with the concentration of all the lives which had been freed from the fallen brave.

Presently came the command, "Front forward!" and the column resumed its direction, straight down upon the centre of the enemy's position on, on it moved with iron nerve.

One hundred Federal guns now concentrated their whole fury of shot and shell upon the advancing line. Every inch of air seemed to be filled with some death-dealing missile. The men and officers were fast being slaughtered. Kemper went down, mangled and bleeding, never again to lead his valiant Virginians in battle.

Up and down the line of his brigade rode Garnett, calling out in his strong voice:

Faster, men, faster! Close up and step out, but don't double-quick!

A long blue line of infantry arose from behind the stone fence, and as the column advanced poured into it a heavy fire of musketry. At once a scattering fire was opened all along the line, when Garnett galloped up and called out: "Cease firing! Save your strength and ammunition!" Under such perfect discipline were these veterans that without slackening their pace they reloaded their guns, shouldered arms, and went on at a quickstep.

The artillery made an effort to support the assault, but the ammunition was almost exhausted. The light pieces which were to have guarded the infantry had been removed to some other part of the field, and none could be found to take their place.

Pettigrew was trying to reach the post of death and honour, but he was far away, and valour could not quite annihilate space. His troops had suffered severely in the battle of the day before and their commander, Heth, had been wounded. They were now led by an officer ardent and brave, but to them unknown.

The four brigades of Archer, Pettigrew, Davis and Brockenbrough deployed from right to left on a single line, a line of battle very difficult to maintain. The left lagged a little; the right, following the gallant Trimble, made heroic efforts to join Pickett whose oblique movement had brought him nearer. Scales and Lane followed Pettigrew.

Dauntlessly Pickett's men pressed forward, the grandest column of heroes that ever made a battlefield glorious. They reached the post-and-rail fence, upon the other side of which, and parallel to it, an ordinary dirt road ran straight through the field across which they were advancing. The fence was but a momentary obstruction. It was but the work of a few seconds to climb over it and into the road, while a hundred blazing cannon poured death-dealing missiles into their devoted ranks.

Now and here was given to the world the grandest exhibition of discipline and endurance, of coolness and courage under a withering fire, ever recorded in military history; a scene which has made the story of Pickett's charge the glory of American arms. There in the road, with the deafening explosion of unnumbered shells filling the air, their ranks ploughed through and through again and again by the fiery hail which the batteries from the heights beyond were pouring into them, amid all this terrific roar and the not less disconcerting cries of the wounded and dying, they heard the command of their company officers:

Halt, men! Form line! Fall in! Right dress!

Imagine, if you can, these heroes reforming and aligning their ranks while their comrades dropped in death-agony about them, the shells bursting above their heads, and an iron storm beating them to the earth. Yet the line was formed, and coolly they awaited the command, "Forward!" At last it came: "Forward! Quick march!" With perfect precision, with all the grace and accuracy of the parade-ground instead of the bloodiest of battlefields, Pickett's division took up its death-march, each man with "the red badge of courage" pinned over his heart. The like was never seen before, and the change in military tactics will prevent its ever being seen again.

Friend and foe looked on in wondering awe. A thrill of admiration held the waiting enemy silent and motionless as they watched this grand and unsurpassable display of Virginia's valour.

As they advanced toward Cemetery Hill there was seen in the open field to the right a long, dark line of men, half a mile distant and at right angles with their line. They were coming at double-quick upon that unprotected right flank, their muskets at right shoulder shift, their banners fluttering in the breeze, their burnished bayonets glistening in the sun. The enemy were strengthening their position, hurrying up reserves from right to left and from opposite directions doubling along the Confederate front.

A heavy rain of shell and shrapnel poured down from the height. In the fiery storm the thin ranks became yet thinner. Not an instant's disorder prevailed, but under the withering fire they marched steadily forward.

"Faster, men, faster! We are almost there!" cried Garnett's clarion voice above the roar of battle. Then he went down among the dead, with the faith of a little child in his hero heart.

There was a muffled tread of armed men from behind, then a rush of trampling feet, and Armistead's brigade from the rear closed up behind the front line. Their gallant leader, with his hat on the point of his sword, took Garnett's place. The division was now four ranks deep. As often as the iron storm made gaps through it the cheer would come from private, corporal, sergeant, lieutenant and captain alike: "Close up! Close up!" and "Forward!" The lines shortened, but never wavered, never halted. Closer and closer they drew to the foe till there remained only a bleeding remnant.

Now they broke forward into a double-quick, while canister and grape whirred and whizzed through the air. On, on, they rushed toward the stone wall where the Federal batteries were pouring forth their deadly missiles. A hundred yards away a flanking force came down on a run, halted suddenly, and fired into the line a deadly storm of musketry. Under this cross-fire they reeled and staggered between falling comrades and the right came pressing down upon the centre, making the line at this point twenty to thirty deep. A few, unable to resist temptation, without orders, faced the enemy on their right, though the latter were sixty to one. The fighting was terrific. Muskets seemed to cross. Men fired to the right and to the front. The fighting was hand-to-hand. The firing was into the enemy's faces.

The Federals in front fell behind their guns to let them belch their grape and canister into the oncoming ranks, piling up the dead and wounded almost in touch of them. When within a few feet of the stone wall the artillery delivered their last fire from the guns shotted to the muzzle.

The division was now in the shape of an inverted V with the point flattened. On it swept over the ground covered with the dead and dying.

Armistead, sword in hand, sprang over the stone wall crying:

Come on, boys, come on! We'll give them the cold steel! Come on! Who will follow me? Who will follow me?

He reached the battery, his hand touched one of Cushing's guns. Then he and Cushing fell together, and a crimson river washed the base of the copse of trees which marked the high tide of the Confederacy—a river formed of the noblest blood that ever flowed in American veins.

Victory was within their grasp. Alas, where were the promised supports? Worn and exhausted by the tension of the bloody fighting of the day before, in which they had suffered terribly, their leaders dead or wounded, they had crumbled away under the deadly hail of the artillery fire.

Back from the flaming crest fell only a remnant of the division which had performed such deeds of valour as made the whole world wonder. The flags which floated a moment ago over Cemetery Hill, lay on the ground among the prostrate forms of the men who had so bravely borne them to the very verge of victory.

Of the five thousand who had followed where the flash of Pickett's sword lit the way to glorious victory, or not less glorious defeat, three thousand five hundred had gone down to the soldier's triumphant death, to live forever in our hearts and on the fame-crowned pages of their country's history.

Virginia is rich in the names of great warriors, statesmen and leaders of men, but the charge of this Virginia division furnishes the most conspicuous proof in the history of the State that the rank and file of its citizen soldiery are the peers of any troops on earth, and the memory of this band of martyrs will be cherished in the hearts of her people forever and forever. With such followers Virginia will never be without great leaders. It was fitting that in the descendants of the great sons of Virginia, who had led in all that had contributed to American grandeur, this consummation of chivalrous manhood should be attained.

The battle-flag of the Confederacy had waved for a moment in triumph to droop forever around its staff. To the South was left the bitter sense of loss, the heartbreak of defeat.

She had left, too, a memory which is enshrined forever in the proudest and grandest niche of her temple of fame, a glorified page of history to thrill the heart of the world while time lingers.

It is the page on which is inscribed the grandest charge known in all the long and proud record of martial history; a charge which will live in song and story while the heart of man can throb responsive to immortal deeds; a charge which can never be obliterated from the roll of fame because, in the changed conditions of warfare, it can never be repeated or equalled; that transcendent charge which awakened echoes to roll through the halls of time and to incite to actions of supernal glory heroes of coming ages—Pickett's charge at Gettysburg.

WHERE WERE THE GUNS?

Where were the guns when Pickett's men started on their grim march to death? is a query which has been often made, and to which

Colonel E. P. Alexander is, perhaps, best fitted to give answer. On this point he says:—

Before daylight on the morning of the third I received orders to post the artillery for an assault upon the enemy's position, and later I learned that it was led by Pickett's division and directed on Cemetery Hill. Some of the batteries had gone back for ammunition and forage, but they were all brought up immediately and by daylight all then on the field were posted. The morning was consumed in waiting for Pickett's division, and possibly other movements of infantry.

While forming for the attack I borrowed from General Pendleton, General Lee's chief of artillery, seven twelve-pound howitzers belonging to the other corps under Major Richardson, which I put in reserve in a selected spot, intending them to accompany Pickett's infantry in the charge, to have the advantage of their horses and men and full chests of ammunition for the critical moment in case the batteries engaged in the preliminary cannonade should be so cut up and exhausted as to be slow in getting up.

For more than half an hour Hill's artillery had a fight for a turn in between the lines; sixty-three guns. Not one of the seventy-five guns which I then had in line was allowed to fire a shot, as we had at best a short supply of ammunition for the work laid out One hundred and thirty to one hundred and fifty rounds are usually carried with each piece, about enough for one hour and a half of rapid firing. Am very sure we did not carry more than one hundred rounds to a gun, and think not over sixty rounds.

About twelve Longstreet told me that when Pickett was ready he would himself give the signal for all our guns to open. He desired

CHARGE OF
ALEXANDER'S ARTILLERY.

me to select a suitable place for reservation, and take with me one of Pickett's staff and exercise my judgement in selecting the moment for Pickett's advance. I selected the salient angle of the wood in which Pickett's line was now formed just on the left flank of my seventy-five guns. Received note from Longstreet:

Headquarters, July 3, 1863.

Colonel: If the artillery fire does not have the effect to drive off the enemy or gradually demoralise him so as to make our efforts pretty certain, I would *prefer that you should* not advise General Pickett to make the charge. I shall rely a great deal on your good judgment to determine the matter, and shall expect you to let General Pickett know when the moment offers. Respectfully,

J. Longstreet, Lieutenant-General.

To Colonel E. P. Alexander,
    Artillery.

General: I will only be able to judge of the effect of our fire on the enemy by his return fire, for his infantry is too little exposed to view, and the smoke will obscure the whole field. If, as I infer from your note, there is any alternative to this attack, it should be carefully considered before opening our fire, for it will take all the artillery ammunition we have left to test this one thoroughly, and if the result is unfavourable we will have none left for another effort. And if this is entirely successful, it can only be so at a very bloody cost.

To this received following reply, which is still in my possession:

Colonel: The intention is to advance the infantry if the artillery has the desired effect of driving the enemy off, or has other effect such as to warrant us in making the attack. When that moment arrives advise General Pickett, but of course advance such artillery as you can use in aiding the attack.

I felt the responsibility very deeply, for the day was rapidly advancing (about twelve or a little later), and whatever was to be done was to be done soon. Meanwhile I had been anxiously discussing the attack with General A. B. Wright, who said that the difficulty was not so much in reaching Cemetery Hill or taking it—his brigade had carried it the afternoon before—but that the trouble was to hold it, for the whole Federal Army was mustered in a sort of horseshoe shape and could rapidly reinforce the point to any extent, while our long enveloping line could not give prompt enough support. This somewhat reassured me, as I had heard it said that morning that General Lee had ordered "every brigade in the army to charge Cemetery Hill," and it was at least certain that the question of supports had had his careful attention.

Before answering I rode back to converse with General Pickett, whose line was now formed or forming in the wood and, without telling him of the question I had to decide, I found out that he was entirely sanguine of success in the charge and was only congratulating himself on the opportunity. I was convinced that to make any halfway effort would ensure a failure of the campaign, and that if our artillery fire was once opened after all the time consumed in preparation for the attack the only hope of success was to follow it up promptly with one extreme effort, concentrating every energy we possessed into it. and my mind was fully made up that *if the artillery opened Pickett must charge*. Wrote to Longstreet:

General: When our artillery fire is doing its best I shall advise General Pickett to advance.

It was my intention, as he had a long distance to traverse, that he should start not later than fifteen minutes after our fire opened. I sent for Richardson with his seven twelve-pounders to come up through the woods and be ready to move ahead of Pickett's division in the advance. To my great disappointment I learned just as we opened fire, and too late to replace him, that General Pendleton had sent four of his guns without my knowledge to some other part of the field, and the other three had also moved off and could not be found. Probably, however, the presence of guns at the head of this column would only have resulted in their loss, but it would have been a brilliant opportunity for them, and I always felt like apologising for their absence."

There have been many efforts to shift responsibility and to assign various causes to this repulse of the Army of Northern Virginia, but I cannot find it in my heart, nor do I think it reasonable, to believe that any man or officer of that grand army, led by the peerless Lee, did aught but what the most profound sense of duty and patriotism, controlled by the emergencies which surrounded him, suggested that he should do.

General Imboden, describing an interview with Lee after the battle, states that in a voice tremulous with emotion, Lee said:

General, I never saw troops behave more magnificently than Pickett's division of Virginians did today in their grand charge upon the enemy. And if they had been supported, as they were to have been—but for some reason, not yet fully explained to me, they were not—we would have held the position they so gloriously won at such a fearful loss of noble lives, and the day would have been ours.

After a moment he added in a tone almost of agony:

Too bad! *Too bad!! Too bad!!!*

A report of the closing scene of the great battle was made by him who was best able to give the true story of Pickett's charge at Gettysburg. It was prepared from notes pencilled on the backs of old letters, on scraps of wrapping-paper, on any fragment large enough to hold a sentence. They were jotted down amid the dead faces bordering the line of retreat, the groans of the wounded and dying, all the fearful sights and sounds of that death-march. They are the memories of a man only a few days away from the most appalling crisis of his life.

This report was suppressed at the request of the commander-in-chief. Weighed down by the responsibility of a great army, Lee shrank from adding to the difficulties of the position by any dissension which might be excited by a bare statement of facts. In a kind and appreciative letter, which has become a part of the published records of the war, admitting the truth of the report, he asked that it might be withdrawn, adding, after setting forth the reasons for his request, the significant words, "We have the enemy to fight."

It was in a spirit of true patriotism that the leader of the Army of Northern Virginia made this request. Those who knew him will remember that of all his many noble utterances none was more impressive than this: "*Duty is the grandest word in human language.*" His duty was to the cause for which he fought, and in the performance of that duty he asked that thin thing might be done. His wishes were respected then, and through all the years that have passed since that time they have not been forgotten. The most alluring temptations have not brought that report from the oblivion to which it was consigned in the far-away past.

The hand which penned those bloodstained notes, reaching from the grave, is as powerful as when it unsheathed the sword upon the field of battle, and it draws across them still the mark of silence. They are all our own—they who went down in the battle-fire, they who left the field with heavy hearts and reluctant steps, longing to stay behind with their comrades who had passed beyond the conflict, our tried and true, our best-beloved. May the soft veil of mercy and love enfold them forever!

Longstreet's Charge at Gettysburg, Pa.
By James I. Metts,

Historical Essay

A certain set of historians, writers and lecturers, who gathered their information from newspapers in Richmond who had their correspondents with the Virginia troops in the army of Northern Virginia during the war—and they so biased as to claim all the glory for the Virginians to the detriment of other troops engaged have so persistently flirted with the truth that those unacquainted with the facts having read their fine descriptions and heard their grand eloquence, accept their statements of Longstreet's, falsely called Pickett's charge, at Gettysburg on the third day, as the truth of history.

Those who love truth rather than fiction, I respectfully refer to the official government diagram of the charge, showing that the Confederate and Federal lines of battle, the stone wall or works of the Federals on Cemetery Ridge, the Emmettsburg road, and the different fences ever which Pettigrew and Trimble's troops had to pass before reaching the works.

To the list of the different troops engaged, taken from war records. Pickett's division, composed of Kemper's, Garnet's and Armistead's brigades, Gen. Kemper's brigade on the right, composed of the following: The First, Third, Seventh, 11th and 24th Virginia regiments. On their left was Garnett's brigade, composed of the following: The Eighth, 18th, 19th, 28th and 56th Virginia regiments. Supporting Kemper and Garnett was Armistead's brigade, *viz:* The 9th, 14th, 38th, 53rd and 57th Virginia regiments. Gen. Heth's division (Gen. Johnston Pettigrew, commanding) formed the left of the line, composed of Archer's, Pettigrew's, Davis' and Brockenbrough's brigades. Archer's brigade, (Col. B. D. Fry, after wound Col. J. G. Shepard, commanding) joined the left of Garnett's brigade, as follows: The 5th and 13th Alabama regiments, and the 1st, 7th and 14th Tennessee regiments.

On their left was Pettigrew's brigade (Col. Marshall, commanding, afterward killed, then by Col. J. Jones), *viz*: The 11th, 26th, 47th and 52nd North Carolina regiments. On their left came Gen. J. R. Davis' brigade *viz*: The 2nd, 11th and 42nd regiments of Mississippi, and the 55th North Carolina regiment. On its left was Gen Brockenbrough's brigade (Col. Robert Mayo, commanding), *viz*: The 40th 47th and 55th Virginia regiments and the 22nd battalion. Supporting Gen Pettigrew's line were Gen. Scales' and Gen. Lane's brigades, (Maj. Gen. L R. Trimble commanding), from Pender's division with Scales' brigade (Col. L. S. J. Lowrance, commanding) on the right, composed of the 13th 16th, 22nd, 38th and 34th North Carolina regiments. On its left was Gen Lane's brigade, *viz*: The 7th, 18th 28th, and 33rd and 37th North Carolina regiments.

(See the War Records, series 1, vol. 87, containing the reports of Maj. J A. Englehard, Ass.-Adj. Gen. Heth's division, (Gen. L. R. Trimble commanding), 556, 552, Col. S. G. Shepard commanding Archer's brigade No. 550. Maj. J. Jones, commanding Pettigrew's brigade No. 553 Brig. Gen. Joseph R. Davis, 558, Brig. Gen. James H. Lane, No. 561 Col. W. L. J. Lowrance commanding, Scales' brigade.)

(Also Moore's *History of North Carolina*, beginning at Page 200, with Gen. Robert E. Lee's report, Brig. Gen. Jas. H. Lane's letter, page 202. Gen. L. R. Trimble's letter, page 203. Jos. H. Sanders' letter, major 33rd North Carolina Infantry W. C. Morris, lieutenant colonel 37th North Carolina Infantry. S. D. Lowe, colonel commanding 28th North Carolina Infantry. E. F. Lovell's, captain 28th North Carolina Infantry. Thomas L. Norwood's captain Company A, 37th infantry. J. McLeod Turner, lieutenant colonel Seventh North Carolina Infantry. Maj. J. G. Harriss and many others.)

From all accounts it appears to have been a very curious line of battle, as Gen. Pickett's divisions started about 100 yards to the west of the Emmettsburg road sheltered by a ridge which Southern troops had occupied the day previous and about 1,000 yards from the enemy's stone wall and works, while Gen. Pettigrew's division, Trimble's division supporting, started from Seminary Ridge (near the artillery), 1,360 yards from the enemy's works. The Emmettsburg road in front of Pettigrew was occupied by Federal troops, and about 100 yards from the works or stone wall also occupied by the Federals. Thus compelling Pettigrew's and Trimble's men to advance in the open field a much greater distance to drive the enemy from the Emmettsburg road and a fence on a line with the low wall in Pickett's front before reaching the stone wall on a small steep slope, which was the height of a man's chin, and 80 yards farther than the wall, about three feet high in Pickett's front, subjecting them to the fearful artillery and infantry fire of the enemy for at least 360 yards further in open field than Pickett's.

They, however, accomplished this, and some men of Archer's, Pettigrew's, Scales' and the left of Garnett's and Armistead's brigades went over the works in the angle where Armistead was killed, while Davis, Lane's and Pettigrew's, with Archer's and Pettigrew's charged to the wall in their front, driving the enemy from behind it, and the cannoneers from their guns, only falling back when flanked by the enemy on both flanks. Brockenbrough's brigade having failed to come up on the left, and Pickett's division to held their position on the right.

Maj. J. A. Englehard, adjutant general of Gen. Pender's division, says:

The point at which the troops with me struck the enemy's works projected farthest to the front. I recollect well, my horse having been shot, I leaned my elbow upon one of the guns of the enemy to rest, and watched with painful anxiety the fight on Pickett's right, for on their success meant the tenableness of our position. Surrounding me were soldiers of Trimble's, of Pettigrew's and of Pickett's division, and it required all the resources at my command to prevent their following *en masse* the retreating enemy, and some did go so far that when we were compelled to withdraw they were unable to reach our lines, the enemy closing in from the right and left. We remained in quiet and undisputed possession of the enemy's work, the men, flushed with victory, eager to press forward.

Col. S. G. Shepard, of Seventh Tennessee regiment, commanding Archer's Brigade, says:

First Tennessee on the right, on its left the 13th Alabama, the 14th and 7th Tennessee and the Fifth Alabama battalion. The space of few hundred yards between Archer's brigade and Picket's division was filled as we advanced and by the time we had gone a little over halfway, by Pickett's bearing to the left. The command was then passed down the line by the officers, 'guide right'! The enemy held their fire until we were in fine range, and opened upon us a terrible and well directed fire.

Within 180 to 200 yards of his works, we came to a lane enclosed by two stout post and plank fences. This was a very great obstruction, but the men rushed over as fast as they could and advanced directly upon the. enemy's works, the first line of which was composed of rough stones. The enemy abandoned this, but just in the rear was massed a heavy force. By the time we had reached this work, our lines all along, as far as I could see, had become very much weakened; indeed, the line, right and left as far as I could observe, seemed to melt away until there was but little left. Those who remained at the works saw it was a hopeless case and fell back.

Archer's brigade remained at the works fighting, as long as any other troops either on the right or left, so far as I could observe. Every flag of the brigade, excepting one, was captured at or within the works of the enemy. The First Tennessee had three colour bearers shot down, the last of whom was at the works, and the flag captured. The 13th Alabama lost three in the same way, the last of whom was shot down at the works. The 14th Tennessee had four shot down, the last of whom was at the works. The Seventh Tennessee had three of her colour bearers killed, the last of whom was at the enemy's works and the flag was only saved by Capt. (A. D.) Norris tearing it away from the staff and bringing it away under his coat. The Fifth Alabama battalion also lost their flag at the enemy's works. There were seven field officers who went into the charge of whom only two came out. The rest were all wounded and captured. The loss in company officers and men was also heavy.

Joseph H. Saunders, the major commanding 33rd North Carolina infantry, says:

I went, by subsequent measure, to within about 60 yards of the stone wall where I was wounded and remained till the next day, when I was taken from the field by the enemy. Just before I was shot, I distinctly remember seeing a Yankee colour bearer just in front of the left of the regiment get up and run away trailing his flag and followed by his regiment; so that there was nothing to keep our regiment from going into the enemy's ranks. I was shot by the troops on the left, mentioned by Gen. Lane in his report. At the time I was, by direction of Col. Avery, acting as left guide to the line of battle, directing the line of march more to the right, so as to strike the enemy's works in a straight line. I see from the Virginian that Capt. Young states Lane and Scales' brigades did not reach the point attained by Pettigrew's. As to this point I can be perfectly positive as we overtook the first line, and the two lines then became one, and the advance was continued. There can be no mistake about this.

Gen. Joseph R. Davis says:

For two hours the artillery fire was heavy and incessant. It (the division) was immediately in the rear of our batteries and with no protection; we suffered some losses. In Davis' brigade two men were killed and 20 wounded. After the artillery ceased the division moved forward, pressing to the right on Pickett's division. Not a shot was fired at us until we reached a strong post and rail fence about three-fourths of a mile from the enemy's position, when we were met by a heavy fire of grape, canister and shell, which told badly upon our ranks.

Under this destructive fire, which commanded our front and left with fatal effect, the troops displayed great coolness, were well in hand and moved steadily forward, regularly closing up the gaps made in their ranks. Our advance across the field was interrupted by other fences of a similar character in crossing which the alignment became more or less deranged. This was in each case promptly rectified and though its ranks were growing thinner at every step, this division 'moved steadily on in line with other troops on the right.

When within musket range, we encountered a heavy fire of small arms, from, which we suffered severely; but this did not for a moment check the advance. The right of the division, owing to the conformation of the ridge on which the enemy was posted, having a shorter distance to pass over to reach his first line of defence, encountered him first in close conflict; but the whole division dashed up to his first line of defence, a stone wall behind which the opposing infantry were strongly posted. Here we were subjected to a most galling fire of musketry and artillery, that so reduced the already thin ranks that further effort to carry the position was hopeless, and there was nothing left to do but retire to the position originally held, which was done in more or less confusion. The coolness of officers and men was worthy of high commendation.

Major J. Jones, commanding Pettigrew's brigade, says:

About 2 o'clock on the third we were ordered to advance. There was an open field in front about three-fourths of a mile wide. In starting off, there was some confusion in the line, owing to the fact that we had been ordered to close in on the right on Pickett's division and that command gave way to the left. This was soon corrected and the distance was made in perfect order. When about half across the intervening space, the enemy opened on us a most destructive fire of grape and canister and when within about 250 or 300 yards of the stone wall behind which the enemy was posted, we were met with a perfect shower of lead from their small arms. The brigade dashed on and many had reached the wall when we were met by a volley from the left. The whole line on the left had given away, and we were being rapidly flanked. With our thinned ranks and in such a position it would have been folly to stand against such odds. We, therefore, fell back to our original position. But one field officer was left in the brigade. Regiments that went in with colonels came out commanded by lieutenants.

Gen. L. R. Trimble says:

When the charge commenced, about 3 p. m., I followed Pettigrew's (Heth's) division, about 150 yards in the rear, a sufficient distance to prevent adverse fire raking both ranks as we marched down the slope. Notwithstanding the losses as we advanced, the men marched with deliberation and accuracy of men on drill. I observed the same in Pettigrew's lines. When the latter was within 150 yards of the Emmettsburg road they seemed to sink I into the earth under the tempest of fire poured into them. We passed; over the remnant of their line, and immediately someone close by my left sung out, 'Three cheers for the Old North State,' when both brigades set up a hearty shout, on which I said to my aid. 'Charley, I believe those fine fellows are going into the enemy's line'.

Lieut. Col. W. C. Morris says:

Soon after we emerged from the woods Davis' brigade, in front of us, became engaged with the enemy, but being exposed to a heavy flanking fire, both of infantry and artillery, was forced to fall back. We were then ordered to double quick. Soon Pettigrew's and Archer's brigades became engaged in front and on our right. About the time Pettigrew's and Archer's brigades became engaged I could see our men on the extreme right falling back. Pettigrew's and Archer's men reached the works a little in advance of us, and succeeded in driving the enemy from his works immediately in their front, but were exposed to a flanking fire both right and left. They laid down, some in the road and some on the crest of the hill near the stone fence, and beckoned to us to come on.

Gen. Trimble then ordered us to charge the enemy's works in our front. The order was promptly obeyed and here Gen. Trimble was wounded. About the time the right of our brigade made this charge, Gen. Lane changed direction to the left, which caused the separation of the Seventh regiment and all on the right of the colours of the 37th in the brigade. We drove the enemy in front of us from his position in the road, then from behind the stone fence and held his position for at least half an hour. Right here, between the road and the stone fence (the enemy having disappeared in our front) we became engaged with a flanking party on our left and were soon surrounded and captured.

Six soldiers on the right of my line were wounded in the enemy's works and captured. Among the number was the lamented Lieut. Battle, whose wound proved fatal. Lieut. Horton was shot through the left lung. I was lieutenant colonel of the 37th regiment. Pettigrew's and Archer's brigades remained longest on our right. Pickett's division did not go further than our command.

Capt. E. F. Lovell says:

I was captain of Company A, 28th North Carolina infantry. Our regiment captured a part of the enemy's works and held them a short time. Some of my men were wounded and captured inside the enemy's works.

Capt. W. R. Bond says:

The Tennessee brigade suffered severely, but the courage of its survivors was unimpaired. There were three Mississippi regiments in Davis' brigade, which between them had 141 men killed on the field. Pickett's dead numbered not quite 15 to the regiment. The five North Carolina regiments of Pettigrew's division bore with fortitude a loss of 229 killed. Pickett's 15th Virginia regiments were fearfully demoralized by a loss of 224 killed. Virginia and North Carolina had each, about the same number of infantry in this battle. Virginia had 375 killed. North Carolina 696. Less than 50 of Pickett's men followed Armistead to the abandoned gun. On July 5, as Lieut. Col. Charles H. Morgan, chief of Gen. Hancock's staff, and Capt. Hazard rode over the field in front of Smythe's brigade, Col. Morgan said to Hazard: 'They may talk as they please about the hard fighting in front of Gibbon, but there are more dead men here than anywhere in our front.' To this conclusion Hazard assented.

The stone wall ran from the left and in front of Lane's, Davis' and Pettigrew's North Carolina brigades and ended where the right of the last named rested at the close of the assault.

Col. L. J. Lowrance, 34th North Carolina Infantry, commanding Scales' brigade, says:

I joined on the right of Gen. Lane's brigade on the second line, under Gen. Trimble's command, in the rear of Pogue's artillery. Here we remained at least an hour, under a most galling fire of artillery, which, I am proud to say, the men endured with the coolness and determined spirit of veterans, for such they are. Then we were ordered forward over a wide, hot and already crimson field of slain. We advanced upon the enemy's line, which was in full view, at a distance of one mile. Now their whole line of artillery was playing on us, which was on an eminence in our front, strongly fortified and supported by infantry. While we were thus advancing many fell, but I saw but few in that hazardous hour who tried to shrink duty. All went forward with a cool and steady step, but ere we had advanced over two-thirds of the way troops from the front came tearing through our ranks, which caused many of our men to break; with the remaining we went forward until the right of the brigade touched the enemy's line of breastworks, as we marched in rather an oblique line. Now the pieces in our front were all silenced. Here many were shot down, being thus exposed to a heavy fire of grape and musketry upon our right flank.

Now all had apparently forsaken us. The two brigades (now reduced to mere squads not numbering in all 800 men) were the only lines to be seen upon that vast field and no support in view. The brigade retreated.

Col. S. D. Lowe, 28th North Carolina Infantry, says:

We advanced about a mile, starting just in rear of Pettigrew's left, which brigade closing and dressing to the right, we to the left, in less than half the distance uncovered us and left our front line over 300 yards from the enemy's works. I received a wound from a minnie ball and was carried to the rear. They were old veterans—true men, and of their own accord would not walk up merely to throw down their guns 'for the war.' I think about one-third of our casualties were killed, the remainder wounded. My men never fought better than on that field.

Lieut. Thomas L. Norwood, Company A, 37th North Carolina regiment, says:

I was first lieutenant, Company A, 37th North Carolina troops, Lane's brigade (Gen. Lane in command), Pender's division (Gen. Trimble commanding). My command, *i.e.*, my own company, and, as far as I observed, the whole regiment and brigade, advanced firmly and cheerfully to within 30 yards of the enemy's works, where he encountered a plank fence. Several officers, myself among the number, sprang over the fence, followed by the whole command, so far as I know. The cannoneers then left their guns. I rushed forward, thinking the day ours, and when within 20 yards of the enemy's works, was called by Lieut. Mickle, who told me that our line had fallen back. Just then he and I, and Lieut. Royster (the only other man that I remember seeing so near the works) were shot down. I know not by whose orders the retreat took place. Mickle and Royster were killed. I was dragged over the breastworks by a Federal sergeant, where I found several prisoners from different commands, but do not know when or how they got there, as I soon fainted.

Capt. D. M. McIntyre, acting adjutant general of Scales' brigade, says:

My brigade went into the enemy's works.

H. L. Guerrant says:

Scales' brigade entered the breastworks and remained there until driven out by the enemy's advancing their flanks. (thus fully sustaining Gen. Trimble and Maj. Englehard).

Gen. James H. Lane says:

My command never moved forward more handsomely. The men reserved their fire in accordance with orders, until within good range of the enemy, and then opening with telling effect, driving the cannoneers from their pieces, completely silencing the guns in our immediate front and breaking the line of infantry on the crest of the hill."

Capt. B. F. Little, Company E, 52nd North Carolina regiment, says:

I was shot when about 50 feet from the enemy's works, and the ground between the enemy's works and where I lay was thickly strewn with killed and wounded, some of them having fallen immediately at the works. I do not think a single one ever got back to the rear, except those who were slightly wounded before they got to the place where I was wounded. And such was the case with the companies on either side of my company. When I was taken prisoner and borne to the rear I passed over their works and found some of my men killed and wounded immediately in the works.

Col. Swallow says:

Pettigrew's brigade, now united with Archer's brigade, which had not entered the fortifications, attacked the enemy with a most desperate determination. While the writer lay wounded with Gen. Smythe of Hays' division, at Gettysburg, that officer told him that Pettigrew's brigade was within 30 feet of his line and fought with a determination that he had never seen equalled. (Gen. Hays' division occupied the left half of the rock wall assaulted on Cemetery Heights).

When Gen. Trimble fell he sent a staff officer to tell Gen Lane he was wounded., and added: 'Tell Lane that if these North Carolinians that I had the honour to lead can't take these works, all hell could not do it.'

Just before Trimble took command of these troops he was a stranger to them and they to him. Their beloved Pender had been carried off the field the day before.

Gen. Lane remained fighting for some time after Pickett left the field. It has been wondered why Pettigrew lost so many more men than Pickett. The answer is this: Every cannon had been dismounted but one piece by the concentrated fire of Alexander's guns in Pickett's front, while in Pettigrew's front were massed three batteries, six guns each, 18 cannon in all. These batteries played sad havoc in Pettigrew's brigade. The grape, canister and shrapnel cut great gaps in their line, but undismayed the men pressed on, climbing two high post fences in the charge to the stone wall. Gen Pettigrew received a grape shot through his left hand, but did not leave the field until the charge had failed. He rode up to Gen. Lee and saluted. Gen. Lee then went to him and asked, him if he was hurt.

When Gen. Pettigrew's division was selected, Gens. Longstreet and Lee thought it had recuperated from the first day's fight, but "they were terribly mistaken," says Col. Venable, of Lee's staff. These troops were very much cut up.

Just before the assault, Gen. Lee rode past Scales' brigade and asked, "What brigade is this?"

Gen. Trimble replied, "It is Scales' North Carolina."

Gen. Lee looked mournfully at the column and said: "I miss many faces here today."

Gen. Scales had been taken off the field in the first day s fight, and every regimental officer. As Lee started off he added, "These poor fellows ought to go to the rear."

Many of them had their heads tied up and their hands tied up as they stood in line. Yet these brave fellows went to the stone wall in the fight and entered the works.

In the charge, Lieut. Col. Gordon, of the 34th North Carolina, and the British Army, but who had united his fortunes with those of the Confederacy was severely wounded before reaching the stone wall and borne from the field. When the litter bearers reached the brigade hospital, Gen. Scales anxiously inquired of Gordon, "How goes the battle. What is the character of the fighting?"

Gordon exclaimed. "The charge at Balaklava is a damned humbug, a damned humbug, sir."

It is said there is a plank in possession of the Pennsylvania Historical Society, taken from the high post fence over which Scales' men charged. This plank is 16 feet long, 14 inches wide and contains 800 bullet holes.

Gen. Longstreet says:

> The signal guns were fired, and all the batteries opened very handsomely and apparently with effective fire. The guns on the hill at the enemy's left (in Pickett's front) were silenced. These at the Cemetery Hill combatted us, however, very obstinately. Many of them were driven off, but fresh ones were brought up to replace them, (these guns were in Pettigrew's and Trimble's front).
>
> Pickett's men were sheltered for some distance, after the advance commenced, with the batteries in their front silenced, while Pettigrew's and Trimble's division caught a fearful fire almost from the start.

Col. Frye, who led Archer's brigade says:

> I heard Garnett give a command. Seeing his gesture of inquiry, I called out, 'I am dressing on you.' A few seconds later he fell dead. A moment later a shot through my thigh prostrated me. The smoke soon became so dense that I could see but little of what was going on on the left (referring to a brigade which had just given away.) All the regimental colours of my command reached the line of the enemy's works, and many of my officers and men were killed while passing over it.

Casualties in Heth's division.

Archer's brigade, Fifth and 13th Alabama, also First. Seventh and 14th Tennessee provisional army, killed 16, wounded 144; total 160.

Pettigrew's brigade, 11th, 26th, 47th, and 52nd North Carolina, killed 190, wounded 915; total 1,105.

Davis' brigade, 55th North Carolina, Second, 11th and 42nd Mississippi, killed 190, wounded 717; total 907.

Brockenbrough's brigade, 22nd, 40th 47th, and 55th Virginia, killed 25, wounded 123; total 148.

Aggregate in Heth's division, killed 421, wounded, 1,899; total 2,320.

Pender's division.

Scales' brigade, 15th, 16th, 32nd, 34th and 58th North Carolina, killed 102; wounded 323; total 425.

Lane's brigade. Seventh, 18th, 28th, 33rd and 57th North Carolina, killed 41; wounded 348; total 389.

McGowan's brigade, First South Carolina (Provisional army) First,

12th, 13th and 14th South Carolina Rifles, killed 100; wounded 477; total 577.

Thomas' brigade, 13th, 30th, 45th and 49th Georgia, killed 16; wounded 136; total 152.

Aggregate of Pender's division, killed 259; wounded 1,284; total 1,543.

Pickett's division.

Kemper's brigade, First, Third, 11th and 24th Virginia, killed 58; wounded 356; total 414.

Armistead's brigade, Ninth, 14th. 38th, 53rd and 57th Virginia, killed 88; wounded 469; total 557.

Garnett's brigade, Eighth, 18th, 19th, 28th and 56th Virginia, killed 78; wounded 324; total 402.

Aggregate Pickett's division, killed 224; wounded 1,149; total 1,373.

Hood's division.

Law's brigade, Fourth, 15th, 44th, 47th and 48th Alabama, killed 74; wounded 276; total 350.

Anderson's brigade Seventh, Ninth, 11th, Eighth and 59th Georgia, killed 105, wounded 512; total 617.

Robertson's brigade, Third Arkansas, First Fourth and Fifth Texas, killed 84; wounded 393; total 477.

Aggregate in Hood's division, killed 263; wounded 1,181; total 1,444.

Losses by brigades, Pettigrew's, Heth's division, 1,105; Davis', 907; Armistead's, Pickett's division, 557; Anderson's, Hoods division, 617; McGowan's, Pender's division, 577.

Casualties Longstreet's charge at Gettysburg. Recapitulation:
Hood's division, three brigades, total killed and wounded 1,444.

Heth's division, four brigades, Pettigrew's 1,105; Archer's 160; Davis' 907; Brockenbrough's 148; total 2,320.

Pender's division, four brigades, McGowan's 577; Thomas' 152; Scales' 425; Lane's 389; total 1,543.

Pickett's division, three brigades, Garnett's 402; Armistead's 557; Kemper's 414; total 1,373.

Hood's division, three brigades, Law's 350; Anderson's 617; Robertson's 477; total 1,444.

Pickett's loss in killed and wounded was less than any other division engaged, and only 268 more than Pettigrew's brigade, while

Heth's division, Gen. Pettigrew commanding, was 947 greater than Pickett's.

Louis C. Young, *aide-de-camp* to Gen. Johnston Pettigrew, says:

When we emerged from the woods into the plains the absence of the two left brigades were discovered, and Gen. Pettigrew instructed me to go for them with all speed, but I had scarcely turned to do so when out came Davis with a rush, but not Brockenbrough's Virginia brigade, and I asked Gen. Pettigrew if I should go for it. He replied 'No.' that it might follow, and if it failed to do so it would not matter. This was a small brigade that had suffered from frequent change or commanders, and had been so badly handled that it was in a chaotic state of demoralization, and was not to be relied upon; it was virtually of no value in a fight. Afterward it advanced to the protection of some rifle pits in front of Seminary Ridge, but it took no part in the charge.

From the evidence produced here of soldiers—aye, heroes—from Tennessee, Mississippi, Alabama and North Carolina, who not only participated in, but advanced to the front as far, some farther, than any of Pickett's, Gen. Longstreet must either have been extremely biased or in total ignorance of the part taken and the heroic fighting by the troops from these States, as his report to Gen. Lee in the war records is very misleading. He extols Pickett and condemns Pettigrew and Trimble's division. Years afterward in his memoirs something came over the spirit of his dream, for his official report must have been a dream of his or his favourite, Gen. Pickett, which caused him to come nearer the facts, though he still evinced very great partiality for Pickett.

He says after Gen. Pickett received his affirmative bow as an order for him to advance his division, Gen. Pickett accepted the duty with seeming confidence of success, leaped on his horse and rode gayly to his command. Gen. Pickett, a graceful horseman, sat lightly in the saddle, his brown locks flowing over his shoulders. Also, that Gen. Pickett, finding the battle broken, while the enemy was still re-enforcing, called the troops off.

New as to the facts: Capt. Lewis G. Young, of Charleston S. C, at the time *aide-de-camp* on Gen. J. J. Pettigrew's staff, says that Gen. Pickett did not lead his men. Capt. Wm. H. Bond, of Scotland Neck, N. C, in his historical essay, "Pickett or Pettigrew," says repeating Gen. Humphreys' invitation to his staff, etc.:

78

Gentlemen, I shall lead this charge. I presume, of course, you will want to ride with me.

Now compare that to Pickett, who was not within a mile of his column when they charged at Gettysburg; Pettigrew and Armistead led Pickett's division there.

Neither Pickett nor any member of his staff, nor even one of his horses, was touched. Why? Because, dismounted, and on the farther side of a hill that protected them from the enemy's fire.

Pettigrew led his division. Pettigrew was wounded by a grape shot shattering his hand, and no member of his staff came out of the fight without being wounded or having his horse shot under him. Gen. Trimble, commanding his division, was severely wounded. Here is further corroborative evidence from one of Gen. Lee's staff, a Virginian, Co. Charles S. Venable, Charlottesville, Va.:

> Wilmington, N. C, March 21. 1899.
> Dear Sir—A few days ago Dr. Isaac Manning suggested that you would probably give me your account of Longstreet's commonly but erroneously called Pickett's charge at Gettysburg. I am collecting data to counteract the falsehoods in regard to that charge, and Dr. Manning thinks your description will be of material assistance. I think he said that Pickett did not lead his men. Respectfully,
>
> James I. Metts.
>
> To Col. Charles S. Venable, Charlottesville, Va.

> Charlottesville, Va., March 22, 1899.
> Dear Sir—Your letter received. My health is not equal to the recapitulating and recalling of the events of the war; I will say all honour can be given to Pickett's brigade, although the general was not with it. Pickett's and Pettigrew's brigade met simultaneously at the brow of the hill at Gettysburg. Pettigrew was well to the front, leading his men. Respectfully,
>
> Chas. S. Venable,
> per M.

Pickett remained behind.

The Civil War, by Frank Moore, contains a description of the battlefield of Gettysburg, etc., by G. J. Cross, who, after describing Longstreet's assault, says:

> In the bloody ruck hundreds of their best officers went down.

It was the turning point of the grand drama, and with the sun, on the 3rd day of July, went down the sun of the 'Confederacy' forever. Although known as Pickett's charge, Gen. Graham, whom I met yesterday, informs me that Pickett himself was not in it. He describes him as a coarse, brutal fellow, and says he treated him with the greatest inhumanity after the battle, whilst wounded and a prisoner in his hands.

John M. Vanderslice says:

As Pickett's division neared the wall it was joined on its left by Frye's Tennessee brigade of Pettigrew's line, and at the same time Lowrance's North Carolina brigade rushed from the rear and joined Frye's and Garnett's at the angle of the wall. The two guns of Cushing's battery at the wall were silenced, and the left of the 71st Pennsylvania was withdrawn to a line with the right, at the all to the rear. Through this gap the Confederates crossed the wall. Garnett had been killed and Kemper wounded. The other guns of Cushing's Battery A, 4th United States, were posted near the clump of trees nearby. Armistead, putting his hat on his sword dashed forward towards the battery, followed by a portion of his command, and fell dead by the side of Cushing, near the 'copse' of woods, which was the extreme point reached by the Confederates in this charge.

Farther to the right, Marshall's brigade, 11th, 26th, 47th and 52nd North Carolina. Davis' 2nd, 11th and 42nd Mississippi, and 55th North Carolina, and Lane's 7th, 18th, 28th, 33rd and 37th North Carolina, were fighting with Smyth's brigade of Hays' division of the Second Corps, 12th New Jersey, 1st Delaware. 14th Connecticut, and 108th New York Infantry and Sherrill's (formerly Willard's) 39th, 111th, 125th and 126th New York Infantry. The two little brigades of Kays' division poured fearful volleys into the brave foe, which compelled some of them to crowd to their right upon Pickett, while others fled or surrendered. Woodruff's battery in the grove to the right, moved forward and swept the enemy with canister. The 8th Ohio, on the skirmish line to the right, changed front forward on left company, and opened fire upon the flank.

The left of the charging column, under Pettigrew and Trimble, suffered as severely as the right, under Pickett.

Great injustice has been done these troops by the prevailing erroneous impression that they failed to advance with those of Pickett. Such is not the fact. As they were formed behind Seminary Ridge, they had over 1,000 yards to march under the terrible fire to which they were exposed, while Pickett's division, being formed under cover of the intermediate ridge had but 900 yards to march under fire. At the first the assaulting columns advanced *en echelon*, but when they reached the Emittsburg road they were on a line. The left of Pettigrew's command becoming first exposed to the fearful enfilading fire upon their left flank from the 8th Ohio and other regiments of Hays' division, and of Woodruff's battery and ether troops, the men on that portion of the line (Brockenbrough's brigade) either broke to the rear or threw themselves on the ground for protection. But Pettigrew's other brigades, Frye's, Davis' and Marshall's, with the brigades of Lowrance and Lane, under Trimble, advanced with Pickett up to the stone wall, and there fought desperately. This is substantiated by the fact that the colours of the 1st and 14th Tennessee and 13th and 5th Alabama were captured at the angle of the wall, and eleven others were picked up between the Emittsburg road and the stone wall, in front of Hays' division. Pettigrew and Trimble, with three of their brigade commanders, Frye, Marshall and Lowrance, were wounded. Davis' brigade lost all its field officers, Marshall's all but one, and Frye's five out of seven.

But why call this Pickett's charge? In this assault there were engaged 12 Confederate regiments. In Pickett's division there were 15 Virginia regiments. In Pettigrew's and Trimble's there were 15 North Carolina; 3 Mississippi; 3 Tennessee; 2 Alabama, and 4 Virginia, the latter being Brockenbrough's brigade. In addition to the artillery fire, they encountered 9 regiments of New York; 5 of Pennsylvania; 3 of Massachusetts; 3 of Vermont; 1 of Michigan; 1 of Maine; 1 of Minnesota; 1 of New Jersey; 1 of Connecticut; 1 of Ohio; 1 of Delaware, 27 in all.

The troops of Trimble's and Pettigrew's divisions behaved as gallantly as those of Pickett. Some prominent writers, even historians like Swinton and Lossing, have said that the left of the line did not advance as was expected, and that it was because the troops were not of the same 'fine quality' as those upon the right; that they were 'raw, undisciplined,' etc. Yet but two days before these same soldiers of Pettigrew and Trimble had fought around Reynold's Grove for six hours, in a single struggle with the First Corps that is unsurpassed for bravery and endurance, and where so many of their number had fallen There were, in fact, no better troops in the Confederate Army than they. Is history repeating itself? If the event is correctly recorded, there were at Thermopylae 300 Spartans, 700 Thespians, and 300 Thebans. It is said the latter went over to the enemy, but the Thespians died, to a man, 'at the pass' with the Spartans. Yet for twenty-three centuries epic song and story have well preserved the memory of the Spartans, while the devoted Thespians are forgotten.

All honour to the Spartan Virginians who, with well-dressed ranks and in splendid array, moved so gallantly, so steadily, so dauntlessly across that death-wept field, but honour, too, the Thespian North Carolinians and other troops who, too, marched and fought there that day. The valour of the one will not be dimmed by according justice to the other.

The rebel corps commanders either did not expose themselves as freely as our own, or they had better luck', for they had none hit, while we lost one, Gen. Reynolds, killed; and two, Hancock and Sickles, wounded. The story told in *Blackwood* by Col. Freemantle, of the British Army, who was present, may help to explain it. He says: 'That carried away by the excitement, he rushed up to Longstreet, who was sitting on a fence, quietly whittling a stick, whilst watching the charge, and said: "Gen. Longstreet, isn't this splendid; I wouldn't have missed it for the world."

"The devil you wouldn't," replied Longstreet; "why, don't you see we are getting licked like hell!"'

Samuel G. Wilkinson, of the North, says:

So terrible was our musketry and artillery fire, that when Armistead's brigade was checked in its charge, and stood reeling, all of its men dropped their muskets and crawled on their hands and knees underneath the stream of shot, till close to our troops, where they made signs of surrendering. They passed through our ranks scarcely noticed, and slowly went down the slope to the road in rear. Before they got there the grand charge of Ewell, solemnly sworn to and carefully prepared, had failed.

Equally or more terrible was that sheet of shot and shell which

82

passed over these magnificent soldiers of Pettigrew's and Trimble's division (for the artillery on their flank had not been silenced) and yet they did not "drop their muskets and crawl to the enemy to surrender"—but like true men, took their chances, and returned to their friends that they might fight another day—for their homes and country.

All honour to the true soldiers of Pickett's, Pettigrew's and Trimble's divisions, who faced that avalanche of shot and shell from the enemy's guns on Cemetery Hill and succeeded—or fell wounded or dead in the charge—in reaching and driving the enemy from his works and guns, and retreated when flanked, taking the chance of being shot, rather than spend the remainder of the war in Northern prisons. All honour to Hoke's North Carolina, and Hay's Louisiana brigades, who captured and held for some time the works in their front at Gettysburg. And the same to Stewart's (George H.) of Johnston's division, who captured the first line of works on Culp's Hill and held it all night and next day, till ordered out. These troops advanced in the open as far and under as heavy fire as any of Longstreet's. All we wish is the truth of history.

James I. Metts,
Captain Company G,
Third North Carolina Infantry
Wilmington, N. C.

CEMETERY RIDGE AFTER PICKETT'S CHARGE, FROM A WAR-TIME SKETCH.

PROFILE OF CEMETERY RIDGE AS SEEN FROM PICKETT'S POSITION BEFORE THE CHARGE.

Lee and Longstreet at High Tide
By Helen D. Longstreet

INTRODUCTION
By Major-General D. E. Sickles, U.S.A.

I am glad to write an introduction to a memoir of Lieutenant-General Longstreet.

If it be thought strange that I should write a preface to a memoir of a conspicuous adversary, I reply that the Civil War is only a memory, its asperities are forgotten, both armies were American, old army friendships have been renewed and new army friendships have been formed among the combatants, the truth of history is dear to all of us, and the amenities of chivalrous manhood are cherished alike by the North and the South, when justice to either is involved. Longstreet's splendid record as a soldier needs neither apologies nor eulogium. And if I venture, further along in this introduction, to defend him from unfair criticism, it is because my personal knowledge of the battle of July 2, 1868, qualifies me to testify in his behalf. It was the fortune of my corps to meet Longstreet on many great fields. It is now my privilege to offer a tribute to his memory. As Colonel Damas says in *The Lady of Lyons*, after his duel with Melnotte, "It's astonishing how much I like a man after I've fought with him."

Often adversaries on the field of battle, we became good friends after peace was restored. He supported President Grant and his successors in their wise policy of restoration. Longstreet's example was the rainbow of reconciliation that foreshadowed real peace Between the North and South. He drew the fire of the irreconcilable South. His statesmanlike forecast blazed the path of progress and prosperity for his people, impoverished by war and discouraged by adversity. He was the first of the illustrious Southern war leaders to accept the result of the great conflict as final. He folded up forever the Confederate flag he had followed with supreme devotion, and thenceforth saluted the Stars and Stripes of the Union with unfaltering homage. He was the trusted servant of the republic in peace, as he had been its relentless foe in war. The friends of the Union became his friends, the enemies of the Union his enemies.

I trust I may be pardoned for relating an incident that reveals the sunny side of Longstreet's genial nature. When I visited Georgia, in March, 1892, I was touched by a call from the general, who came from Gainesville to Atlanta to welcome me to his State. On St. Patrick's Day we supped together as guests of the Irish Societies of Atlanta, at their banquet. We entered the hall arm in arm, about nine o'clock in the evening, and were received by some three hundred gentlemen, with the wildest and loudest "rebel yell" I had ever heard. When I rose to respond to a toast in honour of the Empire State of the North, Longstreet stood also and leaned with one arm on my shoulder, the better to hear what I had to say, and this was a signal for another outburst. I concluded my remarks by proposing,—

Health and long life to my old adversary, Lieutenant-General Longstreet,

. . . . assuring the audience that, although the general did not often make speeches, he would sing the "Star-Spangled Banner." This was, indeed, a risky promise, as I had never heard the general sing. I was greatly relieved by his exclamation:

"Yes, I will sing it!"

And he did sing the song admirably, the company joining with much enthusiasm.

As the hour was late, and we had enjoyed quite a number of potations of hot Irish whiskey punch, we decided to go to our lodgings long before the end of the revel, which appeared likely to last until daybreak. When we descended to the street we were unable to find a carriage, but Longstreet proposed to be my guide; and, although the streets were dark and the walk a long one, we reached my hotel in fairly good form. Not wishing to be outdone in courtesy, I said,—

"Longstreet, the streets of Atlanta are very dark and it is very late, and you are somewhat deaf and rather infirm; now I must escort you to your headquarters."

"All right," said Longstreet; "come on and we'll have another handshake over the bloody chasm."

When we arrived at his stopping-place and were about to separate, as I supposed, he turned to me and said,—

"Sickles, the streets of Atlanta are very dark and you are lame, and a stranger here, and do not know the way back to your hotel; I must escort you home."

"Come along, Longstreet," was my answer.

On our way to the hotel, I said to him,—

"Old fellow, I hope you are sorry for shooting off my leg at Gettysburg. I suppose I will have to forgive you for it someday."

"Forgive me?" Longstreet exclaimed. "You ought to thank me for leaving you one leg to stand on, after the mean way you behaved to me at Gettysburg."

How often we performed escort duty for each other on that eventful night I have never been able to recall with precision; but I am quite sure that I shall never forget St. Patrick's Day in 1892, at Atlanta, Georgia, when Longstreet and I enjoyed the good Irish whiskey punch at the banquet of the Knights of St Patrick.

Afterwards Longstreet and I met again, at Gettysburg, this time as the guests of John Russell Young, who had invited a number of his literary and journalistic friends to join us on the old battlefield. We rode in the same carriage. When I assisted the general in climbing up the rocky face of Round Top, he turned to me and said,—

"Sickles, you can well afford to help me up here now, for if you had not kept me away so long from Round Top on the 2nd of July, 1868, the war would have lasted longer than it did, and might have had a different ending."

As he said this, his stern, leonine face softened with a smile as sweet as a brother's.

We met in March, 1901, at the reception given to President McKinley on his second inauguration. In the midst of the great throng assembled on that occasion Longstreet and I had quite a reception of our own. He was accompanied on this occasion by Mrs. Longstreet. Every one admired the blended courtliness and gallantry of the veteran hero towards the ladies who were presented to him and his charming wife.

At the West Point Centennial Longstreet and I sat together on the dais, near President Roosevelt, the Secretary of War, Mr. Root, and the commander of the army, Lieutenant-General Miles. Here among his fellow-graduates of the Military Academy, he received a great ovation from the vast audience that filled Cullum Hall. Again and again he was cheered, when he turned to me, exclaiming,—

"Sickles, what are they all cheering about?"

"They are cheering you, General," was my reply.

Joy lighted up his countenance, the war was forgotten, and Longstreet was at home once more at West Point.

Again we stood upon the same platform, in Washington, on May 30,—Memorial Day,—1902. Together we reviewed, with President Roosevelt, the magnificent column of Union veterans that marched past the President's reviewing-stand. That evening Longstreet joined me in a visit to a thousand or more soldiers of the Third Army Corps, assembled in a tent near the White House. These veterans, with a multitude of their comrades, had come to Washington to commemorate another Memorial Day in the Capitol of the Nation. The welcome given him by this crowd of old soldiers, who had fought him with all their might again and again, on many battlefields, could hardly have been more cordial if he had found himself in the midst of an equal number of his own command. His speech to the men was felicitous, and enthusiastically cheered. In an eloquent peroration he said:

> I hope to live long enough to see my surviving comrades march side by side with the Union veterans along Pennsylvania Avenue, and then I will die happy.

This was the last time I met Longstreet.

Longstreet was unjustly blamed for not attacking earlier in the day, on July 2, 1863, at Gettysburg. I can answer that criticism, as I know more about the matter than the critics. If he had attacked in the morning, as it is said he should have done, he would have encountered Buford's division of cavalry, five thousand sabres, on his flank, and my corps would have been in his front, as it was in the afternoon. In a word, all the troops that opposed Longstreet in the afternoon, including the Fifth Army Corps and Caldwell's division of the Second Corps, would have been available on the left flank of the Union Army in the morning.

Every regiment and every battery that fired a shot in the afternoon was on the field in the morning, and would have resisted an assault in the morning as stubbornly as in the afternoon. Moreover, if the assault had been made in the morning. Law's strong brigade of Alabamians could not have assisted in the attack, as they did not arrive on the field until noon. On the other hand, if Lee had waited an hour later, I would have been on Cemetery Ridge, in compliance with General

Meade's orders, and Longstreet could have marched, unresisted, from Seminary Ridge to the foot of Round Top, and might, perhaps, have unlimbered his guns on the summit.

General Meade's telegram to Halleck, dated 3 p.m., July 2, does not indicate that Lee was then about to attack him. At the time that despatch was sent, a council of corps commanders was assembled at General Meade's headquarters. It was broken up by the sound of Longstreet's artillery. The probability is that Longstreet's attack held the Union army at Gettysburg. If Longstreet had waited until a later hour, the Union army might have been moving towards Pipe Creek, the position chosen by General Meade on June 30.

The best proof that Lee was not dissatisfied with Longstreet's movements on July 2 is the fact that Longstreet was intrusted with the command of the column of attack on July 3,—Lee's last hope at Gettysburg. Of the eleven brigades that assaulted the Union left centre on July 3, only three of them—Pickett's division—belonged to Longstreet's corps, the other eight brigades belonged to Hill's corps. If Longstreet had disappointed Lee on July 2, why would Lee, on the next day, give Longstreet a command of supreme importance, of which more than two-thirds of the troops were taken from another corps commander?

Longstreet did not look for success on July 3. He told General Lee that "the fifteen thousand men who could make a successful assault over that field had never been arrayed for battle," and yet the command was given to Longstreet Why? Because the confidence of Lee in Longstreet was unshaken; because he regarded Longstreet as his most capable lieutenant.

Longstreet was never censured for the failure of the assault on July 3, although General Lee intimates, in his official report, that it was not made as early in the day as was expected. Why, then, is Longstreet blamed by them for the failure on July 2, when no fault was found by General Lee with Longstreet's dispositions on that day? The failure of both assaults must be attributed to insurmountable obstacles, which no commander could have overcome with the force at Longstreet's disposal,—seventeen thousand men on July 2, and fifteen thousand men on July 3, against thirty thousand adversaries!

In General Lee's official report not a word appears about any delay in Longstreet's movements on July 2, although, referring to the assault of July 3, General Lee says, "General Longstreet's dispositions were not completed as early as was expected." If General Lee did not hesitate to point out unlooked for delay on July 3, why was he silent about delay on July 2? His silence about delay on July 2 implies that there was none on July 2. *Expresio unius exclusio alterius.*

General Lee says, in his report, referring to July 3,—

General Longstreet was delayed by a force occupying the high, rocky hills on the enemy's extreme left, from which his troops could be attacked in reverse as they advanced. His operations had been embarrassed the day previous by the same cause, and he now deemed it necessary to defend his flank and with the divisions of Hood and McLaws.

Another embarrassment prevented an earlier attack on July 2. It was the plan of General Lee to surprise the left flank of the Union Army. General Lee ordered Captain Johnson, the engineer officer of his staff, to conduct Longstreet's column by a route concealed from the enemy. But the formation and movements of the attacking column had been discovered by my reconnaissance; this exposure put an end to any chance of surprise. Other dispositions became necessary; fresh orders from head-quarters were asked for; another line of advance had to be found, less exposed to view. All this took time. These circumstances were, of course, known to General Lee; hence he saw no reason to reproach Longstreet for delay.

The situation on the left flank of the Union Army was entirely changed by my advance to the Emmitsburg road. Fitzhugh Lee says:

Lee was deceived by it and gave orders to attack up the Emmitsburg road, partially enveloping the enemy's left; there was much behind Sickles.

The obvious purpose of my advance was to hold Lee's force in check until General Meade could bring his reserves from his right flank, at Rock Creek, to the Round Tops, on the left. Fortunately for me, General Lee believed that my line from the Peach-Orchard north—about a division front—was all Longstreet would have to deal with. Longstreet soon discovered that my left rested beyond Devil's Den, about twelve hundred yards easterly from the Emmitsburg road, and at a right angle to it. Of course, Longstreet could not push forward to Lee's objective,—the Emmitsburg road ridge,—leaving this force on his flank and rear, to take him in reverse. An obstinate conflict followed, which detained Longstreet until the Fifth Corps, which had been in reserve on the Union right, moved to the left and got into position on the Round Tops. Thus it happened that my salient at the Peach-Orchard, on the Emmitsburg road, was not attacked until six o'clock, the troops on my line, from the Emmitsburg road to the Devil's Den, having held their positions until that hour. The surprise Lee had planned was turned upon himself. The same thing would have happened if Longstreet had attacked in the morning; all the troops that resisted Longstreet in the afternoon—say thirty thousand—would have opposed him in the forenoon.

The alignment of the Union forces on the left flank at 11 a.m., when Lee gave his preliminary orders to Longstreet for the attack, was altogether different from the dispositions made by me at 3 p.m., when the attack was begun. At eleven in the morning my command was on Cemetery Ridge, to the left of Hancock. At two o'clock in the afternoon, anticipating General Lee's attack, I changed front, deploying my left division (Birney's) from Plum Run, near the base of Little Round Top, to the Peach-Orchard, at the intersection of Millerstown and Emmitsburg roads. My right division (Humphrey's) was moved forward to the Emmitsburg road, its left connecting with Birney at the Orchard, and its right *en echelon* with Hancock, parallel with the Codori House.

Longstreet was ordered to conceal his column of attack, for which the ground on Lee's right afforded excellent opportunities. Lee's plan was a repetition of Jackson's attack on the right flank of the Union army at Chancellorsville. In the afternoon, however, in view of the advance of my corps, General Lee was obliged to form a new plan of battle. As he believed that both of my flanks rested on the Emmitsburg road, Lee directed Longstreet to envelop my left at the Peach-Orchard, and press the attack northward "up the Emmitsburg road."

Colonel Fairfax, of Longstreet's staff, says that Lee and Longstreet were together at three o'clock, when the attack began. Lieutenant-General Hill, commanding the First Corps of Lee's army, says in his report,—

> The corps of General Longstreet (McLaws's and Hood's divisions) was on my right, and in a line very nearly at right angles to mine. General Longstreet was to attack the left flank of the enemy, and sweep down his line, and I was ordered to co-operate with him with such of my brigades from the right as could join in with his troops in the attack. On the extreme right. Hood commenced the attack about two o'clock, McLaws about 5.30 o'clock.

Longstreet was not long in discovering, by his artillery practice, that my position at the Peach-Orchard was a salient, and that my left flank really rested twelve hundred yards eastward, at Plum Run, in the valley between Little Round Top and the Devil's Den, concealed from observation by woods; my line extended to the high ground along the Emmitsburg road, from which Lee says:

It was thought our artillery could be used to advantage in assailing the more elevated ground beyond.

General J. B. Hood's story of his part in the battle of July 2, taken from a communication addressed to General Longstreet, which appears in Hood's *Advance and Retreat*, is a clear narrative of the movements of Longstreet's assaulting column. It emphasizes the firm adherence of Longstreet to the orders of General Lee. Again and again, as Hood plainly points out, Longstreet refused to listen to Hood's appeal for leave to turn Round Top and assail the Union rear, always replying:

General Lee's orders are to attack up the Emmitsburg road.

★★★★★★

Hood says:

As soon as I arrived upon the Emmitsburg road I placed one or two batteries in position and opened fire. A reply from the enemy's guns soon developed his lines. His left rested on or near Round Top, with line bending back and again forward, forming, as it were, a concave line, as approached by the Emmitsburg road. A considerable body of troops was posted in front of their main line, between the Emmitsburg road and Round Top Mountain. This force was in line of battle upon an eminence near a peach-orchard.

I found that in making the attack according to orders,—*viz.*, up the Emmitsburg road,—I should have first to encounter and drive off this advanced line of battle; secondly, at the base and along the slope of the mountain, to confront immense boulders of stone, so massed together as to form narrow openings, which would break our ranks and cause the men to scatter whilst climbing up the rocky precipice. I found, moreover, that way division would be exposed to a heavy fire from the main line of the enemy in position on the crest of the high range, of which Round Top was the extreme left, and, by reason of the concavity of the enemy's main line, that we would be subject to a destructive fire in flank and rear, as well as in the front; and deemed it almost an impossibility to clamber along the boulders up this steep and rugged mountain, and, under this number of cross fires, put the enemy to flight I knew that if the feat was accomplished, it must be at a most fearful sacrifice of as brave and gallant soldiers as ever engaged in battle.

I considered it my duty to report to you at once my opinion that it was unwise to attack up the Emmitsburg road, as ordered, and to urge that you allow me to turn Round Top and attack the enemy in flank and rear. Accordingly, I despatched a staff-officer, bearing to you my request to be allowed to make the proposed movement on account of the above stated reasons. Your reply was quickly received: 'General Lee's orders are to attack up the Emmitsburg road.' I sent another officer to say that I feared nothing could be accomplished by such an attack, and renewed my request to turn Round Top.

Again your answer was, 'General Lee's orders are to attack up the Emmitsburg road.' During this interim I had continued the use of the batteries upon the enemy, and had become more and more convinced that the Federal line extended to Round Top, and that I could not reasonably hope to accomplish much by the attack as ordered. In fact, it seemed to me the enemy occupied a position by nature so strong—I may say impregnable—that, independently of their flank fire, they could easy repel our attack by merely throwing and rolling stones down the mountain-side, as we approached.

A third time I despatched one of my staff to explain fully in regard to the situation, and suggest that you had better come and look for yourself. I selected, in this instance, my adjutant-general, Colonel Harry Sellers, whom you know to be not only an officer of great courage, but also of marked ability. Colonel Sellers returned with the same message: 'General Lee's orders are to attack up the Emmitsburg road.' Almost simultaneously, Colonel Fairfax, of your staff, rode up and repeated the above orders.

After this urgent protest against entering the Battle of Gettysburg, according to my instructions,—which protest is the first and only one I ever made during my entire military career,—I ordered my line to advance and make the assault.

As my troops were moving forward, you rode up in person;

a brief conversation passed between us, during which I again expressed the fears above mentioned, and regret at not being allowed to attack in flank around Round Top. You answered to this effect: 'We must obey the orders of General Lee.' I then rode forward with my line under a heavy fire. In about twenty minutes after reaching the Peach-Orchard I was severely wounded in the arm and borne from the field.

With this wound terminated my participation in this great battle. As I was borne off on a litter to the rear, I could but experience deep distress of mind and heart at the thought of the inevitable fate of my brave fellow-soldiers, who formed one of the grandest divisions of that world-renowned army; and I shall ever believe that had I been permitted to turn Round Top Mountain, we would not only have gained that position, but have been able finally to root the enemy.

★★★★★★

These often repeated orders of General Lee to "attack up the Emmitsburg road" could not have been given until near three in the afternoon of July 2, because before that hour there was no Union line of battle on the Emmitsburg road. There had been only a few of my pickets there in the morning, thrown forward by the First Massachusetts Infantry. It distinctly appears that Lee rejected Longstreet's plan to turn the Federal left on Cemetery Ridge. And Hood makes it plain enough that Longstreet refused to listen to Hood's appeal for permission to turn Round Top, on the main Federal line, always replying, "No; General Lee's orders are to attack up the Emmitsburg road." Of course, that plan of battle was not formed until troops had been placed in positions commanding that road. This, we have seen, was not done until towards three in the afternoon.

The only order of battle announced by General Lee on July 2 of which there is any record was to assail my position on the Emmitsburg road, turn my left flank (which he erroneously supposed to rest on the Peach-Orchard), and sweep the attack "up the Emmitsburg road." This was impossible until I occupied that road, and it was then that Longstreet's artillery began its practice on my advanced line.

I am unable to see how any just person can charge Longstreet with deviation from the orders of General Lee on July 2. It is true enough that Longstreet had advised different tactics; but he was a soldier,—a West Pointer,—and once he had indicated his own views, he obeyed the orders of the general commanding,—he did not even exercise the discretion allowed to the chief of a *corps d'armée*, which permits him to modify instructions when an unforeseen emergency imposes fresh responsibilities, or when an unlooked-for opportunity offers tempting advantages.

We have seen that many circumstances required General Lee to modify his plans and orders on July 2 between daybreak, when his first reconnaissance was made, and three o'clock in the afternoon, when my advanced position was defined. We have seen that if a morning attack had been made the column would have encountered Buford's strong division of cavalry on its flank, and that it would have been weakened by the absence of Law's brigade of Hood's division. We have seen that Longstreet, even in the afternoon, when Law had come up and Buford had been sent to Westminster, was still too weak to contend against the reinforcements sent against him. We have seen that Lee was present all day on July 2, and that his own staff-officer led the column of attack. We have seen that General Lee, in his official report, gives no hint of dissatisfaction with Longstreet's conduct of the battle of July 2, nor does it appear that Longstreet was ever afterwards criticised by Lee.

On the contrary, Lee points out that the same danger to Longstreet's flank, which required the protection of two divisions on July 3, existed on July 2, when his flank was unsupported. We have seen that again and again, when Hood appealed to Longstreet for leave to swing his column to the right and turn the Round Tops, Longstreet as often refused, always saying, "No; General Lee's orders are to attack up the Emmitsburg road." The conclusion is irrefutable, that whilst the operations were directed with signal ability and sustained by heroic courage, the failure of both assaults, that of July 2 and the other of July 3, must be attributed to the lack of strength in the columns of attack on both days, for which the commanding general alone was responsible.

It was Longstreet's good fortune to live until he saw his country hold a high place among the great powers of the world. He saw the new South advancing in prosperity, hand in hand with the North, East, and West. He saw his people in the ranks of our army, in Cuba, Porto Rico, the Philippines, China, and Panama; he saw the Union stars and the blue uniform worn by Fitzhugh Lee, and Butler, and Wheeler. He witnessed the fulfilment of his prediction,—that the hearty reunion of the North and South would advance the welfare of both. He lived long enough to rejoice with all of us in a reunited nation, and to know that his name was honoured wherever the old flag was unfurled. His fame as a soldier belongs to all Americans.

Farewell, Longstreet! I shall follow you very soon. May we meet in the happy realm where strife is unknown and friendship is eternal!

THE STORY OF GETTYSBURG

Back of the day that opened so auspiciously for the Confederate cause at the first Manassas, and of the four years that followed, lies Longstreet's record of a quarter of a century in the Union army, completing one of the most lustrous pages in the world's war history. That page cannot be dimmed or darkened; it rests secure in its own white splendour, above the touch of detractors.

The detractors of General Longstreet's military integrity assert that, being opposed to fighting an offensive battle at Gettysburg, he was "balky and stubborn" in executing Lee's orders; that he disobeyed the commanding general's orders to attack at sunrise on the morning of July 2; that, again ordered to attack with half the army on the morning of July 3, his culpably slow attack with only Pickett's division, supported by some of Hill's troops, caused the fatal Confederate defeat in that encounter.

General Gordon has seen fit, in a recent publication, to revive this cruel aspersion.

When General Longstreet surrendered his sword at Appomattox his war record was made up. It stands unassailable—needing no defenders. Back of the day that opened so auspiciously for the Confederate cause at the first Manassas, and of the four years that followed, lies the record of a quarter of a century in the Union Army.

In those times General Longstreet, at Cerro Gordo, Molino del Rey, and Chapultepec, was aiding to win the great empire of the West; in subsequent hard Indian campaigns lighting the fagots of a splendid western civilization, adding new glory to American arms and, in the struggles of a nation that fell, a new star of the first magnitude to the galaxy of American valour, completing one of the most lustrous pages in the world's war history. That page cannot be dimmed or darkened; it rests secure in its own white splendour, above the touch of detractors.

General Longstreet has of late years deemed it unnecessary to make defence of his military integrity, save such as may be found in his memoirs, *Manassas to Appomattox*, published nearly ten years since. He has held that his deeds stand on the impartial pages of the nation's

records—their own defender.

The cold historian of our Civil War of a hundred years hence will not go for truth to the picturesque reminiscences of General John B. Gordon, nor to the pyrotechnics of General Fitzhugh Lee, nor yet to the somewhat hysterical ravings of Rev. Mr. Pendleton and scores of other modern essayists who have sought to fix the failure of Gettysburg upon General Longstreet. The coming chronicler will cast aside the rubbish of passion and hate that followed the war, and have recourse to the nation's official war records, and in the cool, calm lights of the letters and reports of the participants, written at the time, will place the blunder of Gettysburg where it belongs. Longstreet's fame has nothing to fear in that hour.

But for the benefit of the present—of the young, the busy, who have neither time nor inclination to study the records, and for that sentiment that is increasingly shaped by the public press,—for these and other reasons it appears fitting that in this hour historical truth should have a spokesman on the Gettysburg contentions! In the absence of one more able to speak, this little story of the truth is written. The writer belongs to a generation that has come up since the gloom of Appomattox closed the drama of the great "Lost Cause" of American history—a generation that seeks the truth, unwarped and undistorted by passion, and can face the truth.

In the prosecution of my researches for the origin of the extraordinary calumnies aimed at General Longstreet's honour as a soldier, two most significant facts have continually pressed upon my attention.

First, not one word appears to have been published openly accusing him of disobedience at Gettysburg until the man who could forever have silenced all criticism was in his grave—until the knightly soul of Robert Edward Lee had passed into eternity.

Second, General Longstreet's operations on the field of Gettysburg were above the suspicion of reproach until he came under the political ban in the South, for meeting in the proper spirit, as he saw it, the requirements of good citizenship in the observance of his Appomattox parole, and, after the removal of his political disabilities, for having accepted office at the hands of a Republican President who happened to be his old West Point comrade—Grant.

Then the storm broke. He was heralded as traitor, deserter of his people, deserter of Democracy, etc. In the fury of this onslaught originated the cruel slander that he had disobeyed Lee's most vital orders, causing the loss of the Gettysburg battle and the ultimate fall of the Confederate cause. Most singularly, this strange discovery was not made until some years after the battle and General Lee's death. Thereafter for two decades the South was sedulously taught to believe that the Federal victory was wholly the fortuitous outcome of the culpable disobedience of General Longstreet

The sectional complaint that he deserted "Democracy" is about as relevant and truthful as the assertion that he lost Gettysburg. He was a West Pointer, a professional soldier. He had never cast a ballot before the Civil War; he had no politics. Its passions and prejudices had no dwelling-place in his mind. The war was over, and he quietly accepted the result, fraternising with all Americans. It was no great crime.

But the peculiar circumstances favoured an opportunity to make Longstreet the long-desired scape-goat for Gettysburg. There was an ulterior and deeper purpose, however, than merely besmirching his military record. Short-sighted partisans seemingly argued that the disparagement of Longstreet was necessary to save the military reputation of Lee. But Lee's great fame needed no such sacrifice.

The outrageous charges against Longstreet have been wholly disproved. Much of the partisan rancour that once pursued him has died out. Many of the more intelligent Southerners have been long convinced that he was the victim of a great wrong.

It was unworthy of Major-General John B. Gordon, once of the army of Northern Virginia, to revive this dead controversy. He simply reiterates the old charges in full, produces no evidence in their support, and gratuitously endorses a false and cruel verdict. His contribution is of no historical value. It carries inherent evidence that General Gordon made no critical examination of the documentary history of Gettysburg. He assumes to render a verdict on the say-so of others.

Gordon's unsupported assertions would require no attention but for one fact. Both South and North there is a widespread impression that Gordon was a conspicuous figure at Gettysburg. This is erroneous. He was merely a brigade commander there, stationed five miles from Longstreet. It is not certain that he personally saw either Lee or Longstreet while the army was in Pennsylvania.

In his official report Gordon uses this language regarding the operations of his own small command at Gettysburg when the heaviest fighting was going on, finely showing the scope of his opportunities for observation:

The movements during the succeeding days of the battle, July

2 and 3, I do not consider of sufficient importance to mention.

It is but just to Gordon, however, to say that in his subordinate capacity at the head of one of the thirty-seven brigades of infantry comprising Lee's army, he performed excellent service on the first day's battle.

But in estimating his value as a personal witness, the foregoing undisputed facts must be taken into consideration. His testimony is obviously of the hearsay kind. In fact, as will be observed from his own admission, it is no more than his own personal conclusions, wholly deduced from the assertions of others, based on an assumed state of facts which did not exist.

In his recent publication, *Reminiscences of the Civil War*, Gordon says,—

It now seems certain that impartial military critics, after thorough investigation, will consider the following facts established: First, that General Lee distinctly ordered Longstreet to attack early on the morning of the second day, and if Longstreet had done so two of the largest corps of Meade's army would not have been in the fight; but Longstreet delayed the fight until four o'clock in the afternoon, and thus lost his opportunity of occupying Little Round Top, the key of the position, which he might have done in the morning without firing a shot or losing a man.

It is competent to point out that Longstreet's orders from General Lee were "to move around to gain the Emmitsburg road, on the enemy's left." In short, he was "to attack up the Emmitsburg road," as all the authorities agree. He therefore could not well "occupy" Little Round Top up the Emmitsburg road, because it was but a fraction less than a mile to the east of that road. It is as clear as noonday that Lee had no thought at first, if ever, that Little Round Top was the "key to the position." Lee merely contemplated driving the enemy from some high ground on the Emmitsburg road from which the "more elevated ground" of Cemetery Hill in its rear, more than a mile to the northward of Little Round Top, could be subsequently assailed.

Lee's luminous report of the battle, dated July 31, 1863, only four weeks after, has escaped Gordon's notice, or has been conveniently ignored by him. It is found at page 305 *et seq.*, of Part II., Vol. XXVII., of the printed War Records, easily accessible to everybody. At page 308, Lee's report:

. . . In front of General Longstreet the enemy held a position from which, if he could be driven, it was thought our artillery could be used to advantage in assailing the more elevated ground beyond, and thus enable us to reach the crest of the ridge. That officer was directed to carry this position. . . . . After a severe struggle, Longstreet succeeded in getting possession of and holding the desired ground. . . . The battle ceased at dark.

The "desired ground" captured was that held by Sickles's Federal Third Corps,—the celebrated peach-orchard, wheat-field, and adjacent high ground, from which Cemetery Hill was next day assailed by the Confederate artillery as a prelude to Pickett's infantry assault.

It was the "crest of the ridge," not the Round Top, that Lee wished to assail. His eye from the first appears to have been steadily fixed upon the Federal centre. That is why he ordered the "attack up the Emmitsburg road."

Longstreet's official report is very explicit on this point. It was written July 27, 1863. On page 358 of the same book he says—

I received instructions from the commanding general to move, with the portion of my command that was up, around to gain the Emmitsburg road, on the enemy's left.

Lieutenant-General R. H. Anderson, then of Hill's corps, also makes this definite statement:

Shortly after the line had been formed, I received notice that Lieutenant-General Longstreet would occupy the ground on my right, and that his line would be in a direction nearly at right angles with mine, and that he would assault the extreme left of the enemy and drive him towards Gettysburg.

Just here it is pertinent to say that General Longstreet had the afternoon previous, and again that morning, suggested to General Lee the more promising plan of a movement by the Confederate right to interpose between the Federals and their capital, and thus compel General Meade to give battle at a disadvantage. On this point General Longstreet uses the following language in a newspaper publication more than a quarter of a century ago:

When I overtook General Lee at five o'clock that afternoon (July 1), he said, to my surprise, that he thought of attacking General Meade upon the heights the next day. I suggested that this course seemed to be at variance with the plan of the campaign that had been agreed upon before leaving Fredericksburg. He said, 'If the enemy is there tomorrow, we must attack him.' I replied: 'If he is there, it will be because he is anxious that we should attack him—a good reason in my judgment for not doing so.'

I urged that we should move around by our right to the left of Meade and put our army between him and Washington, threatening his left and rear, and thus force him to attack us in such position as we might select. . . . I called his attention to the fact that the country was admirably adapted for a defensive battle, and that we should surely repulse Meade with crushing loss if we would take position so as to force him to attack us, and suggested that even if we carried the heights in front of us, and drove Meade out, we should be so badly crippled that we could not reap the fruits of victory; and that the heights of Gettysburg were in themselves of no more importance to us than the ground we then occupied, and that the mere possession of the ground was not worth a hundred men to us. That Meade's army, not its position, was our objective. General Lee was impressed with the idea that by attacking the Federals he could whip them in detail.

I reminded him that if the Federals were there in the morning it would be proof that they had their forces well in hand, and that with Pickett in Chambersburg, and Stuart out of reach, we should be somewhat in detail. He, however, did not seem to abandon the idea of attack on the next day. He seemed under a subdued excitement which occasionally took possession of him when 'the hunt was up,' and threatened his superb equipoise. . . . When I left General Lee on the night of the 1st, I believed that he had made up his mind to attack, but was confident that he had not yet determined as to when the attack should be made.

★★★★★★

The Campaign of Gettysburg, by Lieutenant-General James Longstreet. One of a series of papers on the Civil War by different distinguished participants, both Union and Confederate, in Colonel A. K. McClure's Philadelphia *Weekly Times,* 1877.

★★★★★★

But General Lee persisted in the direct attack "up the Emmitsburg road." Hood, deployed on Longstreet's extreme right, at once perceived that the true direction was by flank against the southern slopes of Big Round Top. He delayed the advance to advise of the discovery he had made. Soon the positive order came back: "General Lee's orders are to attack up the Emmitsburg road." He still hesitated and repeated the suggestion. Again it was reiterated: "General Lee's orders are to attack up the Emmitsburg road." Then the troops moved to the attack. There was no alternative. Lee's orders were imperative, and made after he had personally examined the enemy's position. Longstreet was ordered to attack a specific position "up the Emmitsburg road," which was *not* Little Round Top, as assumed by Gordon. This point is particularly elaborated because in it lies the "milk in the cocoanut" of the charges against Longstreet.

Without consulting the records Gordon has merely followed the lead of some of General Lee's biographers, notably Fitzhugh Lee, who asserts that his illustrious uncle "expected Longstreet to seize Little Round Top on the 2nd of July." The records clearly show that nothing was farther from General Lee's thoughts.

After the war it was discovered that a very early attack on Little Round Top would perhaps have found it undefended, hence the afterthought that General Longstreet was ordered to attack at sunrise. But whatever the hour Longstreet was ordered to attack, it was most certainly not Little Round Top that was made his objective.

Lee Changes Plan of Campaign

General, I have been a soldier all my life. I have been with soldiers engaged in fights by couples, by squads, companies, regiments, divisions, and armies, and should know as well as anyone what soldiers can do. It is my opinion that no fifteen thousand men ever arrayed for battle can take that position, (pointing to Cemetery Hill).—Longstreet to Lee.

General Longstreet's personal account of this magnificent battle "up the Emmitsburg road" will not be out of place here. In the newspaper article previously quoted from he very graphically describes the advance of the two divisions of McLaws and Hood, for when he went into battle it must be understood that even yet one of his divisions, that of Pickett, was still absent. He states his total force at thirteen thousand men. An account of this dash of arms must send a thrill of pride through every Southern heart:

At half-past three o'clock the order was given General Hood

Major-General D. E. Sickles

to advance upon the enemy, and, hurrying to the head of McLaws's division, I moved with his line. Then was fairly commenced what I do not hesitate to pronounce the best three hours' fighting ever done by any troops on any battlefield. Directly in front of us, occupying the peach-orchard, on a piece of elevated ground that General Lee desired me to take and hold for his artillery, was the Third Corps of the Federals, commanded by General Sickles.

Prompt to the order the combat opened, followed by artillery of the other corps, and our artillerists measured up to the better metal of the enemy by vigilant work. . . . .

In his usual gallant style Hood led his troops through the rocky fastnesses against the strong lines of his earnest adversary, and encountered battle that called for all of his power and skill. The enemy was tenacious of his strong ground; his skilfully handled batteries swept through the passes between the rocks; the more deadly fire of infantry concentrated as our men bore upon the angle of the enemy's line and stemmed the fiercest onset until it became necessary to shorten their work by a desperate charge. This pressing struggle and the crossfire of our batteries broke in the salient angle, but the thickening fire, as the angle was pressed back, hurt Hood's left and held him in steady fight. His right brigade was drawn towards Round Top by the heavy fire pouring from that quarter, Benning's brigade was pressed to the thickening line at the angle, and G. T. Anderson's was put in support of the battle growing against Hood's right.

I rode to McLaws, found him ready for his opportunity, and Barksdale chafing in his wait for the order to seize the battery in his front. Kershaw's brigade of his right first advanced and struck near the angle of the enemy's line where his forces were gathering strength. After additional caution to hold his ranks closed, McLaws ordered Barksdale in. With glorious bearing he sprang to his work, overriding obstacles and dangers. Without a pause to deliver a shot, he had the battery. Kershaw, joined by Semmes's brigade, responded, and Hood's men, feeling the impulsion of relief, resumed their bold fight, and presently the enemy's line was broken through its length.

But his well-seasoned troops knew how to utilise the advantage of their ground and put back their dreadful fires from rocks, depressions, and stone fences, as they went for shelter about Little Round Top. . . . . The fighting had become tremendous, and brave men and officers were stricken by hundreds. Posey and Wilcox dislodged the forces about the Brick House.

General Sickles was desperately wounded!

General Willard was dead!

General Semmes, of McLaws's division, was mortally wounded! I had one brigade—Wofford's—that had not been engaged in the hottest battle. To urge the troops to their reserve power in the precious moments, I rode with Wofford. The rugged field, the rough plunge of artillery fire, and the piercing musket-shots delayed somewhat the march, but Alexander dashed up with his batteries and gave new spirit to the worn infantry ranks. . . . While Meade's lines were growing my men were dropping; we had no others to call to their aid, and the weight against us was too heavy to carry. . . . Nothing was heard or felt but the clear ring of the enemy's fresh metal as he came against us. No other part of the army had engaged! My seventeen thousand against the Army of the Potomac! The sun was down, and with it went down the severe battle.

Surely these are not the utterances of one who had been slow, balky, and obstructive on that field. The ring of these sentences tells no tale of apathy or backwardness because his advice to pursue a different line of operations had been ignored by Lee.

General Gordon, continuing, very complacently assumes that "two of the largest corps of Meade's army would not have been in the fight" of the 2nd had Longstreet attacked early in the morning. He refers to the Union Fifth and Sixth Corps. That statement is correct only as regards the Sixth Corps, which, it is true, did not arrive on the field until late in the afternoon. But it took only a slight part at dark on the 2nd, when the battle was over. Indeed, as it was so slightly engaged, the hour of its arrival at Gettysburg is unimportant. The losses of the different corps conclusively show what part the Sixth, which was the largest in the army, took in the battle of the 2nd of July; as given in the Rebellion Records:

Killed and wounded: First Corps, 3980; Second Corps, 3991; Third Corps, 3662; Fifth Corps, 1976; Sixth Corps, 212; Eleventh Corps, 2353; Twelfth Corps, 1016.

Its non-participation strongly militates against the spirit of Gordon's argument, in that Meade entirely frustrated Lee's plans and defeated the Confederate Army, scarcely using the Sixth Corps, some fifteen thousand men, at all. This is a significant commentary on the anti-Longstreet assumption of how easy it was to win at Gettysburg if only Longstreet had obeyed orders!

At sunrise on the 2nd, the hour at which Longstreet's critics would have had this attack delivered, the Federal Fifth Corps was as near the battle-ground of that day as Longstreet's troops. Longstreet's troops were bivouacked the night previous at Marsh Creek, four miles west of Gettysburg. They began to arrive near Lee's headquarters on Seminary Ridge not earlier than 7 a.m. of the 2nd, and the last of the column did not get in until near noon. Then they were still five miles by the route pursued from the chosen point of attack.

The Union Fifth Corps was bivouacked five miles east of Gettysburg about the same hour on the 1st that Longstreet's tired infantry reached Marsh Creek. At four o'clock a.m. of the 2nd they marched on Gettysburg, arriving about the same hour that Longstreet's troops were being massed near Lee's headquarters, and were thereupon posted upon the extreme Federal right.

Upon the first manifestation of Confederate movements on the right and left, we know that the Fifth Corps was immediately drawn in closer, and about nine o'clock massed at the bridge over Rock Creek on the Baltimore pike, ready for developments. Meade thought Lee intended to attack his right. That Lee contemplated it is quite certain. Colonel Venable, of his staff, was sent about sunrise to consult with Lieutenant-General Ewell upon the feasibility of a general attack from his front. Lee wanted Ewell's views as to the advisability of moving all the available troops around to that front for such a purpose. Venable and Ewell rode from point to point to determine if this should be done. Finally, Venable says, Lee himself came to Ewell's lines, and eventually the design for an attack on the Union right was abandoned.

Where the Fifth Corps was finally massed, it was only one and a half miles in the rear of General Sickles's position. Moreover, it had an almost direct road to that point. This facility for reinforcing incidentally illustrates the advantages of the Union position. At the same hour General Longstreet's troops were still massed near the Chambersburg pike, three miles on a straight line from the point of attack. That is to say, Longstreet had twice as far to march on an air-line to strike Sickles "up the Emmitsburg road" as Sykes had to reinforce the threatened point. But, in fact, Sykes's advantage was far greater in point of time, because, by order of Lee, Longstreet was compelled to move by back

CONFEDERATE PRISONERS ON THE BALTIMORE PIKE, FROM A WAR-TIME SKETCH.

roads and lanes, out of sight of the enemy's signal officers on Round Top. His troops actually marched six or seven miles to reach the point of deployment.

Longstreet eventually attacked about 4 p.m., and the Fifth Corps was used very effectively against him. But no historian who esteems the truth, with the undisputed records before him, will deny that it could and would have been used just as effectively at seven or eight o'clock in the morning. The moment Longstreet's movement was detected it was immediately hurried over to the left and occupied Round Top. If Longstreet had moved earlier, the Fifth Corps also would have moved earlier. It could have been on Sickles's left and rear as early as seven o'clock a.m., had it been necessary. If Ewell and not Longstreet had delivered the general attack it would have been found in his front.

It is mathematically correct to say that the troops which met Longstreet on the afternoon of the 2nd could have been brought against him in the morning. The reports of General Meade, General Sykes, the commander of the Fifth Corps of Sykes's brigade, and regimental commanders, and various other documentary history bearing on the subject, are convincing upon this point.

General Sickles's advance was made in consequence of the Confederate threatening, and would have been sooner or later according as that threatening was made. The critics ignore this fact.

General Longstreet says on this point:

> General Meade was with General Sickles discussing the feasibility of moving the Third Corps back to the line originally assigned for it; the discussion was cut short by the opening of the Confederate battle. If that opening had been delayed thirty or forty minutes, Sickles's corp. would have been drawn back to the general line, and my first deployment would have enveloped Little Round Top and carried it before it could have been strongly manned. The point should have been that the battle was opened too soon.

So much for one part of Gordon's assumption, based upon other assumptions founded upon an erroneous presumption, that if Longstreet had taken wings and flown on an airline from his bivouac at Marsh Creek to the Federal left and attacked at sunrise he would have found no enemy near the Round Tops.

In another equally unwarranted assumption of what the "impartial" military critic will consider an "established fact," Gordon declares:

> Secondly, that General Lee ordered Longstreet to attack at daylight on the morning of the third day, and that the latter did not attack until two or three o'clock in the afternoon, the artillery opening at one.

Lee himself mentions no such order. In his final report, penned six months afterwards, he merely mentions that the "general plan was unchanged," and Longstreet, reinforced, ordered to attack "next morning," no definite hour being fixed. It is significant, however, that in his letter to Jefferson Davis from the field, dated July 4, Lee uses this language:

> Next day (July 3), the third division of General Longstreet's corps having come up, a more extensive attack was made, etc.

The "third division" was Pickett's, which did not arrive from Chambersburg until 9 a.m. of the 3rd. In the same report, Lee himself states that:

> Pickett, with three of his brigades, joined Longstreet the following morning.

There is no dispute, however, about the hour of Pickett's arrival.

So that, as Pickett was selected by Lee to lead the charge, and as Lee knew exactly where Pickett was, it is morally impossible that it was fixed for daylight, five hours before Pickett's troops were up.

In one place Lee remarks in his report:

> The morning was occupied in *necessary* preparations, and the battle recommenced in the afternoon of the 3rd.

Time was not an essential element in the problem of the 3rd. The Federal Army was then all up, whereas Pickett's Confederate division was still absent. The delay of a few hours was therefore a distinct gain for the Confederates, and not prejudicial, as Gordon would have the world believe.

But Longstreet's official report is decisive of the whole question. He says—

> On the following morning (that is, after the fight of the 2nd) our arrangements were made for renewing the attack by my right, with a view to pass round the hill occupied by the enemy's left, and gain it by flank and reverse attack. A few mo-

ments after my orders for the execution of this plan were given, the commanding general joined me, and ordered a column of attack to be formed of Pickett's, Heth's, and part of Pender's divisions, the assault to be made directly at the enemy's main position, the Cemetery Hill.

Clearly this shows that Longstreet had no orders for the morning of July 3. As Longstreet's report passed through Lee's hands, the superior would most certainly have returned it to the subordinate for correction if there were errors in it. This he did not do, neither did Lee indorse upon the document itself any dissent from its tenor.

As Pickett did not come up until 9 a.m., and as General Lee says "the morning was occupied in *necessary* preparations," it was logistically and morally impossible to make an attack at daylight, and General Longstreet states that it could not have been delivered sooner than it was.

Finally, Longstreet emphatically denies that Lee ordered him to attack at daylight on the 3rd. He says that he had no orders of any kind on that morning until Lee personally came over to his front and ordered the Pickett charge. No early attack was possible under the conditions imposed by Lee to use Pickett's, Pettigrew's, and Pender's troops, widely separated.

But without any orders from Lee, as is quite apparent, Longstreet had already given orders for a flank attack by the southern face of Big Round Top, as an alternative to directly attacking again the impregnable heights from which he had been repulsed the night before. That would have been "simple madness," to quote the language of the Confederate General Law. But such an act of "simple madness" was the only daylight attack possible from Longstreet's front on the morning of the 3rd. Lee substituted for the feasible early attack projected by Longstreet the Pickett movement straight on Cemetery Heights which it required hours of preparation to fulminate, and which proved the most disastrous and destructive in Confederate annals. It was, in fact, the death-knell of the Southern republic.

In his published memoirs, (*From Manassas to Appomatox*), General Longstreet makes this concise statement in regard to Lee's alleged orders for the early morning operations on the 3rd:

He (General Lee) did not give or send me orders for the morning of the third day, nor did he reinforce me by Pickett's brigades for morning attack. As his headquarters were about four miles from the command, I did not ride over, but sent, to report the work of the second day. In the absence of orders, I had scouting parties out during the night in search of a way by which we might strike the enemy's left and push it down towards his centre. I found a way that gave some promise of results, and was about to move the command when he (Lee) rode over after sunrise and gave his orders.

But in his paper of 1877, on Gettysburg, hereinbefore freely quoted from, General Longstreet goes more into detail with relation to Lee's plans and orders for the morning of the 3rd, and more fully discloses the genesis of the Pickett charge. In this account his own opposition to a renewal of the attack on Cemetery Hill is developed and the obvious reasons therefor. As he is confirmed in nearly every particular by participants and by the records, his account is here reprinted:

On the next morning he came to see me, and, fearing that he was still in his disposition to attack, I tried to anticipate him by saying, 'General, I have had my scouts out all night, and I find that you still have an excellent opportunity to move around to the right of Meade's army and manoeuvre him into attacking us.' He replied, pointing with his fist at Cemetery Hill, 'The enemy is there, and I am going to strike him.' I felt then that it was my duty to express my convictions. I said, 'General, I have been a soldier all my life. I have been with soldiers engaged in fights by couples, by squads, companies, regiments, divisions, and armies, and should know as well as anyone what soldiers can do. It is my opinion that no fifteen thousand men ever arrayed for battle can take that position,' pointing to Cemetery Hill.
General Lee, in reply to this, ordered me to prepare Pickett's division for the attack. I should not have been so urgent had I not foreseen the hopelessness of the proposed assault. I felt that I must say a word against the sacrifice of my men; and then I felt that my record was such that General Lee would or could not misconstrue my motives. I said no more, however, but turned away. The most of the morning was consumed in waiting for Pickett's men and getting into position.

To make the attitude of the superior and his subordinate more clear in relation to the proposed desperate throw of General Lee for victory, and to further explain the foregoing protest of General Longstreet, quotations from a second paper of the series printed in 1877 are here given, in which he says—

In my first article I declared that the invasion of Pennsylvania was a movement that General Lee and his council agreed should be defensive in tactics, while of course it was offensive in strategy; that the campaign was conducted on this plan until we bad left Chambersburg, when, owing to the absence of our cavalry and our consequent ignorance of the enemy's whereabouts, we collided with them unexpectedly, and that General Lee had lost the matchless equipoise that usually characterized him, and through excitement and the doubt that enveloped the enemy's movements, changed the whole plan of the campaign and delivered a battle under ominous circumstances.

PICKETT'S CHARGE

Pickett swept past our artillery in splendid style, and the men marched steadily and compactly down the slope. As they started up the ridge over one hundred cannon from the breastworks of the Federals hurled a rain of canister, grape and shell down upon them; still they pressed on until halfway up the slope, when the crest of the hill was lit with a solid sheet of flame as the masses of infantry rose and fired. When the smoke cleared away Pickett's division was gone. Nearly two-thirds of his men lay dead on the field.—Longstreet on Pickett's Charge.

General Longstreet's description of the Pickett charge itself also throws much light on these old controversies. It is confirmed in all essential particulars by General Alexander and others who have written on the subject since the war, and also by the reports:

The plan of assault was as follows: Our artillery was to be massed in a wood from which Pickett was to charge, and it was to pour a continuous fire upon the cemetery. Under cover of this fire, and supported by it, Pickett was to charge. General E. P. Alexander, a brave and gifted officer, being at the head of the column, and being first in position, and being besides an officer of unusual promptness, sagacity, and intelligence, was given charge of the artillery. The arrangements were completed about one o'clock. General Alexander had arranged that a battery of seven 11-pound howitzers, with fresh horses and full caissons, were to charge with Pickett, at the head of his line, but General Pendleton, from whom the guns had been borrowed, recalled them just before the charge was made, and thus deranged this wise plan.

Never was I so depressed as upon that day. I felt that my men were to be sacrificed, and that I should have to order them to make a hopeless charge. I had instructed General Alexander, being unwilling to trust myself with the entire responsibility, to carefully observe the effect of the fire upon the enemy, and when it began to tell to notify Pickett to begin the assault. I was so much impressed with the hopelessness of the charge that I wrote the following note to General Alexander:

'If the artillery fire does not have the effect to drive off the enemy or greatly demoralise him, so as to make our efforts pretty certain, I would prefer that you should not advise General Pickett to make the charge. I shall rely a great deal on your judgment to determine the matter, and shall expect you to let Pickett know when the moment offers.'

To my note the general replied as follows:

'I will only be able to judge the effect of our fire upon the enemy by his return fire, for his infantry is but little exposed to view, and the smoke will obscure the whole field. If, as I infer from your note, there is an alternative to this attack, it should be carefully considered before opening our fire, for it will take all of the artillery ammunition we have left to test this one thoroughly, and if the result is unfavourable, we will have none left for another effort, and even if this is entirely successful it can only be so at a very bloody cost.'

I still desired to save my men, and felt that if the artillery did not produce the desired effect I would be justified in holding Pickett off. I wrote this note to Colonel Walton at exactly 1.30 p.m.:

'Let the batteries open. Order great precision in firing. If the batteries at the peach-orchard cannot be used against the point we intend attacking, let them open on the enemy at Rocky Hill.'

The cannonading which opened along both lines was grand. In a few moments a courier brought a note to General Pickett (who was standing near me) from Alexander, which, after reading, he handed to me. It was as follows:

'If you are coming at all you must come at once, or I cannot give you proper support; but the enemy's fire has not slackened at all; at least eighteen guns are still firing from the cemetery itself.'

After I had read the note Pickett said to me, 'General, shall I advance?' My feelings had so overcome me that I would not speak for fear of betraying my want of confidence to him. I bowed affirmation and turned to mount my horse. Pickett immediately said, 'I shall lead my division forward, sir.' I spurred my horse to the wood where Alexander was stationed with artillery. When I reached him he told me of the disappearance of the seven guns which were to have led the charge with Pickett, and that his ammunition was so low that he could not properly support the charge. I at once ordered him to stop Pickett until the ammunition had been replenished. He informed me that he had no ammunition with which to replenish. I then saw that there was no help for it, and that Pickett must advance under his orders. He swept past our artillery in splendid style, and the men marched steadily and compactly down the slope.

As they started up the ridge over one hundred cannon from the breastworks of the Federals hurled a rain of canister, grape, and shell down upon them; still they pressed on until half-way up the slope, when the crest of the hill was lit with a solid sheet of flame as the masses of infantry rose and fired. When the smoke cleared away Pickett's division was gone. Nearly two-thirds of his men lay dead on the field, and the survivors were sullenly retreating down the hill. Mortal man could not have stood that fire. In half an hour the contested field was cleared and the Battle of Gettysburg was over.

When this charge had failed I expected that of course the enemy would throw himself against our shattered ranks and try to crush us. I sent my staff-officers to the rear to assist in rallying the troops, and hurried to our line of batteries as the only support that I could give them, knowing that my presence would impress upon every one of them the necessity of holding the ground to the last extremity. I knew if the army was to be saved those batteries must check the enemy."

Gordon's "Established Facts" and Pendleton's Fulminations

No officer in a position to know anything about the matter confirmed Pendleton's statement, while everybody who should have been aware of such an important order directly contradicted it, as do all the records.

Continuing on the subject of Longstreet's alleged disobedience, Gordon considers the following as another of the "facts established:"

Thirdly, that General Lee, according to the testimony of Colonel Walter Taylor, Colonel C. S. Venable, and General A. L. Long, who were present when the order was given, ordered Longstreet to make the attack on the last day with the three divisions of his own corps and two divisions of A. P. Hill's corps, and that instead of doing so Longstreet sent only fourteen thousand men to assail Meade's army in the latter's strong and heavily entrenched position.

This is the old story that Longstreet was culpable in not sending McLaws and Hood to the attack with Pickett.

But, in fact, Lee's own utterances show that McLaws and Hood were not to join in the Pickett attack, but, on the contrary, were excluded for other vital service by Lee's specific directions. It is true this was done upon Longstreet's strenuous representations that twenty thousand Federals were massed behind the Round Top to swoop down on the Confederate flank if Hood and McLaws were withdrawn. After viewing the ground himself Lee acquiesced. The eye-witnesses quoted by Gordon heard only the original order; they evidently did not know of its necessary modification, after Lee was made aware by his own personal observations and by Longstreet's explanations that it was impossible to withdraw Hood and McLaws.

The official reports of both Lee and Longstreet are conclusive on this point, and they substantially agree. In the paragraph quoted in the preceding chapter, Longstreet states explicitly that "the commanding general joined me" (on the far right on the morning of the 3rd) "and ordered a column of attack to be formed of Pickett's, Heth's, and part of Pender's divisions," *etc.* If this, was a misstatement, why did not Lee correct it before sending the report to the War Department? He did not; on the contrary, Lee corroborates Longstreet in these paragraphs of his own official report, in which he also explains in detail why McLaws and Hood were not ordered forward with Pickett:

General Longstreet was delayed by a force occupying the high rocky hills on the enemy's extreme left, from which his troops could be attacked in reverse as they advanced. His operations had been embarrassed the day previous by the same causey and he now deemed it necessary to defend his flank and rear with the divisions of Hood and McLaws. He was therefore reinforced

116

by Heth's division and two brigades of Pender's. . . . . General Longstreet ordered forward the column of attack, consisting of Pickett's and Heth's divisions in two lines, Pickett on the right.

Now, one of Lee's favourite officers, General Pickett, had personal supervision of the formation of the attaining column. General Lee was for a time personally present while this work was going on, conversing with Pickett concerning the proper dispositions and making various suggestions. He therefore knew by personal observation, before the charge was made, exactly what troops were included and what were not. He knew that the extreme right of Hood's division was at that moment fully three miles away, holding a difficult position in face of an overwhelming force of Federals, and McLaws almost equally distant.

With these documents before him, how can Gordon believe it an "established fact" that Lee expected McLaws and Hood to take part in the Pickett charge?

It is admitted by almost if not quite all authority on the subject that Pickett's charge was hopeless. The addition of McLaws and Hood would not have increased the chances of success. The Confederates under Longstreet and R. H. Anderson had tested the enemy's position on that front thoroughly in the battle of the 2nd, and with a much larger force, including these same divisions of McLaws and Hood, who had been repulsed. There was every reason to believe that the position was much stronger on the final day than when Longstreet attacked it on the 2nd.

The troops of Hood and McLaws, in view of their enormous losses, were in no condition to support Pickett effectively, even had they been free for that purpose. But it has been shown above by the testimony of both Lee and Longstreet that they were required to maintain the position they had won in the desperate struggle of the evening previous to prevent the twenty-two thousand men of the Union Fifth and Sixth Corps from falling en masse upon Pickett's right flank, or their own flank and rear had they moved in unison with Pickett.

Having proved from Lee's own official written utterances that the three foregoing points set up by Gordon cannot possibly be accepted as "established facts," we now come to his "fourthly," which is really a summing up of the whole case against Longstreet—viz., that he was disobedient, slow, "balky," and obstructive at Gettysburg. He says—

Fourthly, that the great mistake of the halt on the first day would have been repaired on the second, and even on the third day, if Lee's orders had been vigorously executed, and that General Lee died believing that he lost Gettysburg at last by Longstreet's disobedience of orders.

The first positive utterance holding General Longstreet responsible for the defeat at Gettysburg, through failure to obey Lee's orders, came from Rev. Dr. William N. Pendleton, an Episcopal clergyman of Virginia, on the 17th of January, 1878. General Lee had then been dead more than two years. In view of what follows it is well to bear in mind these two distinct dates. There had been some vague hints, particularly among some of the higher ex-Confederates from Virginia prior to Pendleton's categorical story, but Pendleton was the first person to distinctly formulate the indictment against Longstreet for disobedience of orders. In an address delivered in the town of Lexington, Virginia, on the date mentioned, in behalf of a memorial church to General Lee, Pendleton uses this language, referring to the Battle of Gettysburg:

> The ground southwest of the town (Gettysburg) was fully examined by me after the engagement of July 1. . . . . . Its practicable character was reported to our commanding general. He informed me that he had *ordered Longstreet to attack am that front at sunrise next morning.* And he added to myself: 'I want you to be out long before sunrise, so as to re-examine and save time.' He also desired me to communicate with General Longstreet, as well as himself. The reconnaissance was accordingly made as soon as it was light enough on the 2nd. . . . All this, as it occurred under my personal observation, it is nothing' short of imperative duty that I thus fairly state.

Rev. Dr. Pendleton was a brigadier-general and chief of artillery on Lee's staff. He was a graduate of West Point, and was the cadet friend of Lee for more than three years in the Military Academy. After the war they were closely associated at Lexington, Virginia. His fulmination had the effect of a bombshell. There was a hue and cry at once; corroborative evidence of the easy hearsay sort was forthcoming from various interested quarters, but most markedly and noisily from the State of Virginia, as if by preconcert. Pendleton's fulmination appeared to have been expected by those who had previously been pursuing Longstreet. The late General Jubal A. Early was particularly strenuous in unreserved endorsement of the Pendleton story. The Rev. J. William

Jones, of Richmond, the self-appointed conservator of General Lee's fair fame, also quickly added his testimony to the reliability of the Rev. Dr. Pendleton's discovery and dramatic disclosure. Those who approved generally fortified Pendleton with additional statements of their own.

Pendleton's statement is characteristic of the whole, but it was for a time the more effective because it was more definite, in that it purported to recite a positive statement by Lee of an alleged order to Longstreet. If Pendleton's statement falls, the whole falls.

General Longstreet was astounded when Pendleton's Lexington story was brought to his attention. He had previously paid but little attention to indefinite gossip of a certain coterie that he had been "slow" and even "obstructive" at Gettysburg, and had never heard before that he was accused of having disobeyed a positive order to attack at any given hour. That false accusation aroused him to action. He categorically denied Pendleton's absurd allegations, and at once appealed to several living members of Lee's staff and to others in a position to know the facts, to exonerate him from the charge of having disobeyed his chief, thereby causing disaster.

Colonel Walter H. Taylor, a Virginian, and General Lee's adjutant-general, promptly responded as follows:

Norfolk, Virginia, April 28, 1875.
Dear General,—I have received your letter of the 20th inst. I have not read the article of which you speak, nor have I ever seen any copy of General Pendleton's address; indeed, I have read little or nothing of what has been written since the war. In the first place, because I could not spare the time, and in the second, of those of whose writings I have heard I deem but very few entitled to any attention whatever. I can only say that I never before heard of 'the sunrise attack' you were to have made as charged by General Pendleton. If such an order was given you I never knew of it, or it has strangely escaped my memory. I think it more than probable that if General Lee had had your troops available the evening previous to the day of which you speak he would have ordered an early attack, but this does not touch the point at issue. I regard it as a great mistake on the part of those who, perhaps because of political differences, now undertake to criticise and attack your war record. Such conduct is most ungenerous, and I am sure meets

the disapprobation of all good Confederates with whom I have had the pleasure of associating in the daily walks of life.

Yours very respectfully,

W. H. Taylor

To General Longstreet.

Two years afterwards Colonel Taylor published an article strongly criticising General Longstreet's operations at Gettysburg, but in that article was this candid admission:

Indeed, great injustice has been done him (Longstreet) in the charge that he had orders from the commanding general to attack the enemy at sunrise on the 2nd of July, and that he disobeyed these orders. This would imply that he was in position to attack, whereas General Lee but anticipated his early arrival on the 2nd, and based his calculations upon it. I have shown how he was disappointed, and I need hardly add that the delay was fatal.

The fact that Colonel Taylor was himself a somewhat severe critic of General Longstreet, through a misapprehension of certain facts and conditions, gives additional force and value to this statement.

Colonel Charles Marshall, then an *aide* on Lee's staff, who succeeded Long as Military Secretary and subsequently had charge of all the papers left by General Lee, wrote as follows:

Baltimore, Maryland, May 7, 1875.

Dear General,—Your letter of the 20th *ult.* was received and should have had an earlier reply but for my engagements preventing me from looking at my papers to find what I could on the subject. I have no personal recollection of the order to which you refer. It certainly was not conveyed by me, nor is there anything in General Lee's official report to show the attack on the 2nd was expected by him to begin earlier, except that he notices that there was not proper concert of action on that day. . . .

Respectfully,

Charles Marshall.

To General Longstreet, New Orleans.

Colonel Charles S. Venable, another of Lee's *aides* and after the war one of his firmest partisans, made the following detailed statement, which not only refutes Pendleton's Lexington story, but bears luminously upon every other point at issue concerning the alleged early-attack order of the 2nd:

University of Virginia, May 11, 1875.

General James Longstreet:

Dear General,—Your letter of the 25th *ultimo*, with regard to General Lee's battle order on the 1st and 2nd of July at Gettysburg, was duly received. I did not know of any order for an attack on the enemy at sunrise on the 2nd, nor can I believe any such order was issued by General Lee. About sunrise on the 2nd of July I was sent by General Lee to General Ewell to ask him what he thought of the advantages of an attack on the enemy from his position. (Colonel Marshall had been sent with a similar order on the night of the 1st.) General Ewell made me ride with him from point to point of his lines, so as to see with him the exact position of things.

Before he got through the examination of the enemy's position General Lee came himself to General Ewell's lines. In sending the message to General Ewell, General Lee was explicit in saying that the question was whether he should move all the troops around on the right and attack on that side. I do not think that the errand on which I was sent by the commanding general is consistent with the idea of an attack at sunrise by any portion of the army.

Yours very truly,

Chas. S. Venable.

General A. L. Long, a Virginian, was General Lee's Military Secretary and *aide* at Gettysburg. After the war he wrote a book—*Memoirs of General Lee*—in which he endeavoured to hold Longstreet largely responsible for the Gettysburg disaster. But in it he made no assertion that Longstreet had disobeyed an order for a sunrise attack on the 2nd, or at any other specific hour on that or the next day. He wrote as follows:

Big Island, Bedford, Virginia, May 31, 1875.

Dear General—Your letter of the 20th *ult.*, referring to an assertion of General Pendleton's, made in a lecture delivered several years ago, which was recently published in *the Southern Historical Society Magazine* substantially as follows: 'That General Lee ordered General Longstreet to attack General Meade at sunrise on the morning of the 2nd of July,' has been received. I do not recollect of hearing of an order to attack at sunrise, or at any other designated hour, pending the operations at Gettysburg during the first three days of July, 1863. . . .

Yours truly,

A. L. Long

To General Longstreet.

The foregoing letters, all written by members of General Lee's military family, all his close friends and personal partisans, are worth a careful study. They not only negative General Pendleton's "sunrise" story, but as a whole they go to prove that it was not expected by Lee, Longstreet, Pendleton, nor any other high officer, that an early attack was to have been delivered on the 2nd of July. Both Generals McLaws and Hood, Longstreet's division commanders, made statements disclosing that they were totally unaware at Gettysburg of any order for a sunrise attack on that day. No officer in a position to know anything about the matter confirmed Pendleton's statement, while everybody who should have been aware of such an important order, directly contradicted it, as do all the records.

The statement of General McLaws appeared in a narrative of Gettysburg published in a Savannah paper nearly thirty years ago. Besides its direct bearing on the Pendleton story, it furnishes valuable information as to some of the causes of delay encountered by Longstreet's troops in their long march from Chambersburg on the 1st of July:

On the 30th of June I had been directed to have my division in readiness to follow General Ewell's corps. Marching towards Gettysburg, which it was intimated we would have passed by ten o'clock the next day (the 1st of July), my division was accordingly marched from its camp and lined along the road in the order of march by eight o'clock the 1st of July. When the troops of Ewell's corps (it was Johnston's division in charge of Ewell's wagon-trains, which were coming from Carlisle by the road west of the mountains) had passed the head of my column I asked General Longstreet's staff-officer. Major Fairfax. if my division should follow. He went off to inquire, and returned with orders for me to wait until Ewell's wagon-train had passed, which did not happen until after four o'clock p.m.

The train was calculated to be fourteen miles long, when I took up the line of march and continued marching until I arrived within three miles of Gettysburg, where my command camped along a creek. This was far into the night. My division was leading Longstreet's corps, and of course the other divisions came up later. I saw Hood's division the next morning, and understood that Pickett had been detached to guard the rear.

While on the march, at about ten o'clock at night I met General Longstreet and some of his staff coming from the direction of Gettysburg and had a few moments' conversation with him. He said nothing of having received an order to attack at daylight the next morning. Here I will state that until General Pendleton mentioned it about two years ago, when he was on a lecturing tour, after the death of General Lee, I never heard it intimated even that any such order had ever been given."

The following is an extract from a letter of General Hood to General Longstreet on the subject of the sunrise order, (see note following), which indirectly, though conclusively, shows there could have been no such order, besides being interesting and instructive as to other points:

I arrived with my staff in front of the heights of Gettysburg shortly after daybreak, as I have already stated, on the morning of the 2nd of July. My division soon commenced filing into an open field near me, when the troops were allowed to stack arms and rest until further orders. A short distance in advance of this point, and during the early part of the same morning, we were both engaged in company with Generals A. P. Hill and Lee in observing the position of the Federals. General Lee, with coat buttoned to the throat, sabre belt around his waist, and field-glasses pending at his side, walked up and down in the shade of large trees near us, halting now and then to observe the enemy. He seemed full of hope, yet at times buried in deep thought. Colonel Fremantle, of England, was ensconced in the forks of a tree not far off with glasses in constant use examining the lofty position of the Federal Army.

General Lee was seemingly anxious that you should attack that morning. He remarked to me, 'The enemy is here, and if we do not whip him he will whip us.' You thought it better to await the arrival of Pickett's division, at that time still in the rear, in order to make the attack, and you said to me subsequently, while we were seated together near the trunk of a tree, 'General

Lee is a little nervous this morning. He wishes me to attack. I do not wish to do so without Pickett. I never like to go into a battle with one boot off.'"

★★★★★★

Note:—See *Advance and Retreat*, General J. B. Hood's Biography. It is from this letter that I obtain the information concerning Hood's proposed flank movement on Round Top. It was General Hood's letter which informed historians that "General Lee's orders are to attack up the Emmitsburg road." See Hood's letter as to this; also that of Colonel Fairfax in this work.

★★★★★★

Another letter, which in a way is still more important than any of the foregoing, is one from Colonel John W. Fairfax, a member of General Longstreet's staff. It tends to show that the sunrise-order story was conjured up by Dr. Pendleton and others at Lexington after Lee's death; in other words, it is strong circumstantial confirmation of General Longstreet's belief in a conspiracy. Written more than twenty-six years ago, the manner in which it dovetails with all the foregoing statements and documents as to the various events involved is peculiarly significant. Colonel Fairfax is a Virginian and was always an ardent admirer of General Lee, but not to the extent of desiring to uphold his fame at the expense of honour or the ruin of another:

Freestone P. O., Prince William County, Virginia.
November 12, 1877.

My Dear General Longstreet—.....The winter after the death of General Lee I was in Lexington, visiting my sons at the Virginia Military Institute. General Pendleton called to see me at the hotel. General Custis Lee was in my room when he came in. After General Lee left. General Pendleton asked me if General Longstreet was not ordered to attack on the 2nd of July at six o'clock in the morning, and did not attack until four in the evening. I told him it was not possible. When he left me I was under the impression I had convinced him of his mistaken idea. I told General Pendleton that you and General Lee were together the greater part of the day up to about three o'clock or later; that you separated at the mouth of a lane not long thereafter. You said to me, 'Those troops will be in position by the time you get there; tell General Hood to attack.'

When I gave the order to General Hood he was standing within a step or two of his line of battle. I asked him to please delay his attack until I could communicate to General Longstreet that he can turn the enemy—pointing to a gorge in the mountain, where we would be sheltered from his view and attack by his cavalry. General Hood slapped me on the knee, and said, 'I agree with you; bring General Longstreet to see for himself. When I reported to you, your answer was, 'It is General Lee's order; the time is up—attack at once.' I lost no time in repeating the same to General Hood, and remained with him to see the attack, which was made instantly. We had a beautiful view of the enemy's left from Hood's position, which was close up to him. He gave way quickly. General Hood charged, and I spurred to report to you; found you with hat in hand, cheering on General McLaws's division. . . . .

Truly your friend,

John W. Fairfax.

General Longstreet's views at the time of the Gettysburg operations are conveyed in a personal letter of a confidential nature, written only twenty days after the event to his uncle in Georgia, upon being made aware that there was a sly undercurrent of misrepresentation of his course current in certain circles of the army:

Camp Culpepper Court-House,
July 24, 1863.

My Dear Uncle—Your letters of the 13th and 14th were received on yesterday. As to our late battle I cannot say much.
I have no right to say anything, in fact, but will venture a little for you alone. If it goes to aunt and cousins it must be under promise that it will go no farther. The battle was not made as I would have made it. My idea was to throw ourselves between the enemy and Washington, select a strong position, and force the enemy to attack us. So far as is given to man the ability to judge, we may say with confidence that we should have destroyed the Federal Army, marched into Washington, and dictated our terms, or at least held Washington and marched over as much of Pennsylvania as we cared to, had we drawn the enemy into attack upon our carefully chosen position in his rear. General Lee chose the plans adopted, and he is the person appointed to choose and to order. I consider it a part of my duty to express my views to the commanding general.

If he approves and adopts them, it is well; if he does not, it is my duty to adopt his views and to execute his orders as faithfully as if they were my own. I cannot help but think that great results would have been obtained had my views been thought better of, yet I am much inclined to accept the present condition as for the best. I hope and trust that it is so. Your programme would all be well enough had it been practicable, and was duly thought of, too. I fancy that no good ideas upon that campaign will be mentioned at any time that did not receive their share of consideration by General Lee. The few things that he might have overlooked himself were, I believe, suggested by myself.

As we failed, I must take my share of the responsibility. In fact, I would prefer that all the blame should rest upon me. As General Lee is our commander, he should have the support and influence we can give him. If the blame, if there is any, can be shifted from him to me, I shall help him and our cause by taking it. I desire, therefore, that all the responsibility that can be put upon me shall go there and shall remain there. The truth will be known in time, and I leave that to show how much of the responsibility of Gettysburg rests on my shoulders. . . . .

Most affectionately yours,

J. Longstreet.

To A. B. Longstreet, LL.D., Columbus, Ga.

Aside from all this irrefragable personal testimony of conspicuous participants disproving Pendleton's apocryphal story, there is other evidence still more conclusive that no sunrise order for attack by Longstreet was given by Lee, and equally strong that an early attack on that day was out of the question. The position of Longstreet's troops, all still absent from the field and on the march, forbade an attack by him at sunrise, or at any other hour much before noon, at the point designated by Lee. General Lee was well aware of its impossibility. At sunrise Longstreet's infantry was still distant from the field, but rapidly coming up. One brigade (Law's) was not less than twenty miles away at the very hour Pendleton would have had Longstreet attack. McLaws's and Hood's divisions had encamped at Marsh Creek, four miles from Gettysburg, at midnight of the 1st, and did not begin to arrive on Seminary Ridge until more than three hours after sunrise on the 2nd.

The corps artillery did not get up until nine or ten o'clock, and part of it not until noon or after. Pickett's division did not begin its march from the vicinity of Chambersburg, some thirty miles away, until the 2nd. Pendleton's report, herein quoted, shows how the artillery was delayed, and the deterrent effect that delay had upon Longstreet's advance after he received the order. Pendleton himself was the chief of artillery, and largely responsible for its manoeuvres.

After their arrival upon Seminary Ridge, the infantry of Hood and McLaws was massed in a field within musket shot of General Lee's headquarters, and there rested until the troops took arms for the march to the point of attack. From this point of rest near Lee's head-quarters to the point of attack, by the circuitous route selected by Pendleton, was between five and seven miles.

So that Longstreet's infantry, the nearest at hand, had from nine to eleven miles to march to reach the selected point of attack, the greater part of which march by the back roads and ravines, to avoid the observation of the enemy, was necessarily slow at best, and made doubly so by the mistakes of Pendleton's guides, who put the troops upon the wrong routes. The artillery, still back on the Chambersburg road, did not all get up until noon, causing a further delay of the whole column, as shown by the Pendleton report. General Law's brigade, marching from 3 a.m., arrived about noon.

After they came up all movements were still several hours delayed, awaiting Lee's personal reconnoissances on the left and right to determine the point of attack.

Colonel Venable says that "about sunrise" he was sent to General Ewell on the left to inquire if it were not more feasible to attack in that quarter. While he was riding from point to point with Ewell, Lee himself came over to see Ewell in person. Lee did not return to Longstreet's front until about nine o'clock. Meanwhile, his staff officers, Pendleton, Long, Colonel Walker, and Captain Johnston, by Lee's orders, had been examining the ground to the right. Upon Lee's return from the left he rode far to the right and joined Pendleton.

Not until then was the attack on the enemy's left by Longstreet finally decided upon. Longstreet said it was not earlier than eleven o'clock when he received his orders to move; from the time consumed by Lee and his staff it was probably later. The front of the Confederate Army was six miles in extent.

Hence matters on the morning of July 2 were not awaiting Longstreet's movements. All that long forenoon everything was still in the air, depending upon Lee's personal examinations and final decisions.

It is perfectly clear from this indecision on the 2nd that Lee could not have arrived at a decision the previous night, as asserted by Pendleton at Lexington long after the war.

Longstreet's Version of the Operations of July 2

General Lee never in his life gave me orders to open an attack at a specific hour. He was perfectly satisfied that when I had my troops in position and was ordered to attack no time was ever lost.—Longstreet on the Second Day at Gettysburg.

The hour, the feasibility, and point of attack have now been thoroughly discussed, mainly from the standpoint of the official records. As supplementary to the recitations of the official reports of Lee, Longstreet, Pendleton, and others quoted on these heads, it seems desirable to introduce just here General Longstreet's version of his operations on July 2, published so long ago as 1877, only twelve years after Appomattox and two decades before he knew the tenor of Pendleton's report. It was given to the world long before the publication of the official records by the government, to which he could therefore have had no access. How closely he is confirmed in all essential particulars by the records is marvellous. In this regard it is to be noted that in all these controversies his statements have always stood analysis in the light of all the evidence far better than those of his reckless critics. The following is useful because it comprehensively sums up from Longstreet's stand-point all the movements relating to fixing the point and time of his attack, the movement and disposition of his troops, and other incidents:

General Lee never in his life gave me orders to open an attack at a specific hour. He was perfectly satisfied that when I had my troops in position and was ordered to attack, no time was ever lost. On the night of the 1st I left him without any orders at all. On the morning of the 2nd I went to General Lee's headquarters at daylight and renewed my views against making an attack. He seemed resolved, however, and we discussed the probable results. We observed the position of the Federals and got a general idea of the nature of the ground. About sunrise General Lee sent Colonel Venable, of his staff, to General Ewell's headquarters, ordering him to make a reconnaissance of the ground in his front, with a view of making the main attack on his left. A short time afterwards he followed Colonel Venable in person.

128

Second day's Battle, Gettysburg

He returned at about nine o'clock and informed me that it would not do to have Ewell open the attack. He finally determined that I should make the main attack on the extreme right. It was fully eleven o'clock when General Lee arrived at this conclusion and ordered the movement. In the meantime, by General Lee's authority. Law's brigade, which had been put upon picket duty, was ordered to rejoin my command, and upon my suggestion that it would be better to await its arrival, General Lee assented. We waited about forty minutes for these troops and then moved forward.

A delay of several hours occurred in the march of the troops. The cause of this delay was that we had been ordered by General Lee to proceed cautiously upon the forward movement so as to avoid being seen by the enemy. General Lee ordered Captain Johnston, of his engineer corps, to lead and conduct the head of the column. My troops therefore moved forward under guidance of a special officer of General Lee, and with instructions to follow his directions. I left General Lee only after the line had stretched out on the march, and rode along with Hood's division, which was in the rear. The march was necessarily slow, the conductor frequently encountering points that exposed the troops to the view of the signal station on Round Top. At length the column halted.

After waiting some time, supposing that it would soon move forward, I sent to the front to inquire the occasion of the delay. It was reported that the column was awaiting the movements of Captain Johnston, who was trying to lead it by some route by which it could pursue its march without falling under view of the Federal signal station. Looking up towards Round Top, I saw that the signal station was in full view, and, as we could plainly see this station. It was apparent that our heavy columns were seen from their position and that further efforts to conceal ourselves would be a waste of time.

I became very impatient at this delay, and determined to take upon myself the responsibility of hurrying the troops forward. I did not order General McLaws forward because, as the head of the column, he had direct orders from General Lee to follow the conduct of Colonel Johnston. Therefore, I sent orders to Hood, who was in the rear and not encumbered by these instructions, to push his division forward by the most direct route so as to take position on my right. He did so, and thus broke up the delay. The troops were rapidly thrown into position and preparations were made for the attack.

We had learned on the night of the 1st, from some prisoners captured near Seminary Ridge, that the First, Eleventh, and Third Corps had arrived by the Emmitsburg road and had taken position on the heights in front of us, and that reinforcements had been seen coming by the Baltimore road just after the fight of the 1st. From an intercepted despatch we learned that another corps was in camp about four miles from the field. We had every reason, therefore, to believe that the Federals were prepared to renew the battle. Our army was stretched in an elliptical curve, reaching from the front of Round Top around Seminary Ridge, and enveloping Cemetery Heights on the left; thus covering a space of four or five miles.

The enemy occupied the high ground in front of us, being massed within a curve of about two miles, nearly concentric with the curve described by our forces. His line was about fourteen hundred yards from ours. Anyone will see that the proposition for this inferior force to assault and drive out the masses of troops upon the heights was a very problematical one. My orders from General Lee were 'to envelop the enemy's left and begin the attack there, following up as near as possible the direction of the Emmitsburg road.'

My corps occupied our right, with Hood on the extreme right and McLaws next. Hill's corps was next to mine, in front of the Federal centre, and Ewell was on our extreme left. My corps, with Pickett's division absent, numbered hardly thirteen thousand men. I realized that the fight was to be a fearful one; but being assured that my flank would be protected by the brigades of Wilcox, Perry, Wright, Posey, and Mahone, moving *en echelon*, and that Ewell was to co-operate by a direct attack on the enemy's right, and Hill to threaten his centre and attack if opportunity offered, and thus prevent reinforcements from being launched either against myself or Ewell, it seemed that we might possibly dislodge the great army in front of us.

PENDLETON'S REPORT

Pendleton's report will destroy many illusions of Lee's misguided friends who are unwittingly doing deadly injury to his military fame by magnifying the mistakes of Gettysburg and ascribing them to another.—Leslie J. Perry, formerly of the War Records Department.

There is even more positive proof than has yet been produced. That Lee gave no such order as described in Pendleton's Lexington lecture, or for an "early attack," as asserted by Gordon now, is absolutely proved by an official report of Gettysburg, penned by General Pendleton himself. That Pendleton was an oral falsifier of history is established by his own hand, under date of September 12, 1863, only nine weeks after the battle.

Confident in his own rectitude of purpose and conduct, and far from being an expert controversialist, for he was without guile himself, it is not at all singular that the significance of Pendleton's report in connection with the Lexington story should for years have entirely escaped General Longstreet's notice. He knew that the document was printed in its sequence in the Gettysburg volumes of the War Records, and for certain purposes had even quoted from it regarding other questions. He was also fully aware that General Pendleton had long been distinguished for the unreliability of his memory. Nevertheless General Longstreet had never analysed the report to the extent of observing that it made ridiculous the reverend gentleman's version of 1873.

It is most striking that the extraordinary tenor of this old Pendletonian exhumation of the War Records office in Washington should so long have passed entirely unnoticed by everybody, despite the researches of the most industrious. It remained for Mr. Leslie J. Perry, one of the historical experts then in charge of the government publication of the Union and Confederate records of the Civil War, to point out some nine years ago how glaringly the Pendleton report of 1863 stultified the Pendleton story of 1873.

The immediate result of the exploitation of the Pendleton report was the elimination of the sunrise story from the repertory of the anti-Longstreet crusaders. In the subsequent literature of the subject a decided change of tone regarding other allegations was soon perceived, more favourable to Longstreet. General Longstreet was astounded by this bald disclosure of his old military associate's tergiversation, to call it nothing worse. For a time after the appearance of the Lexington story, he had charitably presumed that, in an excess of zeal to protect General Lee's military fame, Pendleton might really have harboured in good faith the belief that his Lexington statements were true. But after reading the detailed analysis of the Pendleton report, and carefully studying the report itself. General Longstreet speedily arrived at the conclusion that he was the victim of a deliberate conspiracy. It is not strange that he found it hard to forgive the conspirators, even after becoming fully aware that the world was practically convinced that he had been cruelly misrepresented.

Let us see how "fairly" Pendleton stated the case against General Longstreet in his Lexington lecture. His official report of Gettysburg was written only about sixty days after the battle. It was dated September 12, 1868. (For General Pendleton's official report, see Part II., Vol. XXVII., War Records. That is the volume in which will he found all the other Confederate reports referred to in the text). It is a detailed report of the operations of the Confederate artillery in the Pennsylvania campaign, embodying a minute description of General Pendleton's personal movements on that day. That is its only value to this discussion. The paragraphs having a bearing upon the time of Longstreet's attack are as follows:

> From the farthest occupied point on the right and front, in company with Colonels Long and Walker and Captain Johnston (engineer), soon after sunrise I surveyed the enemy's position towards some estimate of the ground and best mode of attack. So far as judgment could be formed from such a view, assault on the enemy's left by our extreme right might succeed, should the mountain there offer no insuperable obstacle. The attack on that side, if practicable, I understood to be the purpose of the commanding general.
>
> Returning from this position more to the right and rear, for the sake of tracing more exactly the mode of approach, I proceeded some distance along the ravine road noticed the previous evening, and was made aware of having entered the enemy's lines by meeting two armed dismounted cavalrymen. Apparently surprised, they immediately surrendered, and were disarmed and sent to the rear.
>
> Having satisfied myself of the course and character of this road, I returned to an elevated point on the Fairfield road, which furnished a very extensive view, and despatched messengers to General Longstreet and the commanding general. This front was, after some time, examined by Colonel Smith and Captain

Johnston (engineers), and about midday General Longstreet arrived and viewed the ground. He desired Colonel Alexander to obtain the best view he then could of the front. I therefore conducted the colonel to the advanced point of observation previously visited. Its approach was now more hazardous from the fire of the enemy's sharp-shooters, so that special caution was necessary in making the desired observation. Just then a sharp contest occurred in the woods to the right and rear of this forward point.

Anderson's division, Third Corps, had moved up and was driving the enemy from these woods. These woods having thus been cleared of the enemy, some view of the ground beyond them, and much farther to the right than had yet been examined, seemed practicable. I therefore rode in that direction, and when about to enter the woods, met the commanding general *en route* himself to survey the ground.

There being here still a good deal of sharp-shooting, the front had to be examined with caution. . . . . Having noticed the field and the enemy's batteries, *etc.*, I returned to General Longstreet for the purpose of conducting his column to this point, and supervising, as might be necessary, the disposition of his artillery. He was advancing by the ravine road (as most out of view), time having already been lost in attempting another, which proved objectionable because exposed to observation. On learning the state of facts ahead, the general halted, and sent back to hasten his artillery.

Members of my staff were also despatched to remedy, as far as practicable, the delay. Cabell's, Alexander's, and Henry's battalions at length arrived, and the whole column moved towards the enemy's left. . . . The enemy opened a furious cannonade, the course of which rendered necessary a change in the main artillery column. Cabell's deflected to the left, while Alexander's was mainly parked for a season, somewhat under cover, till it could advance to better purpose. . . . Soon after, at about 4 p.m., the general assault was made.

Here is the whole of Pendleton's celebrated report, so far as it bears upon the hour of Longstreet's attack on the 2nd of July. Nothing is omitted relating to the preliminary movements of Longstreet's column of attack, or that in any manner modifies the tenor of the parts introduced.

Pendleton's Unreliable Memory

All the battle worthy the name for the Southern cause at Gettysburg on the 2nd and 3rd was made by Longstreet. The whole superstructure of the contentions against his honour as a soldier is based solely on the statements since the war, and since Lee's death, of two or three obscure individuals. They are easily exploded by the records of the battles; they are corroborated by none.

When the Rev. Dr. Pendleton told that dramatic story to his breathless hearers at Lexington in 1873, under "pressure of imperative duty," had he forgotten the tenor of his official report, made in 1863? The story as modified by the prior report forms the greatest anti-climax in all history. Several decisive facts are disclosed by this unbiased report.

1. Instead of being dilatory and obstructive, Pendleton himself establishes that Longstreet was personally exerting himself to "hasten forward" the very artillery of which he, Pendleton, was the chief.

2. As late certainly as eleven o'clock, if not noon, General Lee and his staff-officers were still rambling an over a front six miles long, yet undetermined either as to the point or proper route of attack. According to both Pendleton and Venable, they did not *begin* this necessary preliminary survey until "about sunrise," the specific hour at which General Lee on the night previous had already ordered Longstreet to begin his attack, as asserted by Pendleton at Lexington.

3. Not until Lee and Pendleton had devoted the entire forenoon to the examination of the ground, did Pendleton go to conduct Longstreet to the point of attack thereupon decided upon. Evidently Longstreet was not delaying action; he was awaiting their motions. The following general conclusions upon the state of facts disclosed by Pendleton's, remarkable report are therefore inevitable and unavoidable.

1. At sunrise of the 2nd, General Lee himself did not know where to attack. He did not know as late as ten or eleven o'clock. His mind was not fully made up until after he came back from Ewell's front (about nine o'clock, according to all authorities), and had made the final examination on the right.

General Longstreet says he received his orders to move about eleven o'clock, and this corresponds with Pendleton's report. But if anything, it was later, rather than earlier.

2. These painstaking, time-consuming reconnoiasances of the commanding general and his staff-officers, the journey of Colonel Venable to Ewell, three miles to the left, and Lee's later visit to Ewell, together with the unavoidable absence of General Longstreet's troops until late in the morning, prove absolutely that Lee issued no order for Longstreet to attack at any specific hour on July 2.

3. Longstreet's preliminary movements from start to finish were under the personal supervision of Lee's confidential staff-officer, Pendleton, and the subordinate staff officers. So Longstreet has positively stated, so has General McLaws, and both are confirmed by Pendleton's report. The staff guide caused a loss of three hours by putting the head of McLaws's column upon a wrong road. This compelled Longstreet to "hasten matters" by assuming personal direction of the movement, and pushing Hood's division rapidly to the front past McLaws.

4. Pendleton's official utterances make it an "established fact" that General Longstreet made his tremendous and successful attack on July 2 at the earliest moment possible after receiving Lee's orders to advance, under the conditions imposed by Lee,—*viz.*, to be conducted to the point of attack by Pendleton himself and the other staff-officers.

Thus the misapprehensions respecting Longstreet's great part at Gettysburg were cleared away, and a better general understanding of what actually occurred was obtained from the Rev. Mr. Pendleton's report of September 12, 1863. Few military students now hold that Longstreet was in the remotest degree culpable for Lee's defeat. On the contrary, most of them severely criticise Lee's operations from start to finish, particularly the hopeless assaults he persisted in making, and for the lack of concert. It is held generally now that the dreadful result fully justified Longstreet's protests against attacking the Federals in that position, and that his suggestion of a turning movement was far more promising of success.

In all the circumstances it is not only entirely improbable, but the developed facts of the battle make it impossible that "General Lee died believing that he lost Gettysburg at last by Longstreet's disobedience of orders." Longstreet disobeyed no orders at Gettysburg, and Lee was well aware of the fact. General Gordon has simply reiterated the claque set up after Lee's death by his fond admirers to shift the responsibility of defeat from his shoulders upon Longstreet. It was necessary to the success of that folly to make the world believe Lee always quietly held that view, and only imparted it in the strictest confidence to close friends like the ex-army chaplain. Rev. J. William Jones, and the Rev. William N. Pendleton.

The evidence is totally insufficient. Its gauzy character is fully exposed by the Pendleton report. But apocryphal after-war evidence of this kind was the only reliance of the conspirators. It is absolutely certain that there is no evidence of any such belief in any of Lee's official utterances during the progress of the war, nor a hint of it in his private correspondence then or afterwards, so far as has been produced. The whole superstructure of the contention is based solely on the statements since the war, and since Lee's death, of two or three obscure individuals. Pendleton's Lexington yam is an example. They are easily exploded by the records of the battle; they are corroborated by none. All the battle worthy the name for the Southern cause at Gettysburg on the 2nd and 3rd was made by Longstreet.

Another evidence of the falsehoods concerning Longstreet's disobedience and Lee's alleged belief is found in the relations of the two men. Their personal friendship continued after Gettysburg as it was before. It was of the closest and most cordial description. General Lee always manifested the highest regard for General Longstreet, and continued to manifest undiminished confidence in his military capacity, fighting qualities, and subordination. There is no manifestation of a withdrawal of that confidence after Gettysburg. I here cite a few illustrations of their relations after Gettysburg. Just after his corps was ordered to reinforce Bragg before Chattanooga, Longstreet wrote Lee from Richmond, where he had temporarily stopped on his journey to the new field:

> If I did not think our move a necessary one, my regrets at leaving you would be distressing to me. . . . Our affections for you are stronger, if it is possible for them to be stronger, than our admiration for you.

After the Battle of Chickamauga Lee wrote to Longstreet:

> . . . . . My whole heart and soul have been with you and your brave corps in your late battle. . . . Finish the work before you,

Retreat from Gettysburg (Accident during the night-crossing of the Potomac on a pontoon bridge)

my dear General, *and return to me. I want you badly, and you cannot get back too soon.*

These letters, printed in the, official records, were written less than ninety days after the battle of Gettysburg.

"I want you badly" does not indicate that Longstreet had ever failed General Lee. They are significant words, so soon after the event wherein Longstreet, by mere obstinacy and obduracy, had defeated his chief's plans, if we may believe Gordon, Pendleton, and Jones. After the forlorn campaign in East Tennessee against overwhelming numbers, when General Longstreet was on his way back to the Army of Northern Virginia with his troops to aid in repelling Grant, Lee's adjutant-general wrote him as follows at Gordonsville or Orange Court-House:

> Headquarters Army of Northern Virginia,
> April 26, 1864.
>
> My dear General,—I have received your note of yesterday and have consulted the general about reviewing your command. He directs me to say that he has written to the President to know if he can visit and review the army this week, and until his reply is received, the General cannot say when he can visit you. He is anxious to see you, and it will give him much pleasure to meet you and your corps once more. He hopes soon to be able to do this, and I will give you due notice when he can come. I really am beside myself, General, with joy of having you back. It is like the reunion of a family.
>
> Truly and respectfully yours,
>
> W. H. Taylor, A.A.G.
>
> To General Longstreet.

After the war was over and the Southern cause lost, there are warm letters from General Lee, written before Longstreet had accepted appointment at the hands of a Republican President. A few months after the surrender General Lee wrote:

> If you become as good a merchant as you were a soldier I shall be content. No one will then excel you, and no one can wish you more success and more happiness than I. My interest and affection for you will never cease, and my prayers are always offered for your prosperity.

Lexington Va: 19 Jan '66

My dear Sir

Upon my return from Richmond, where I have been for a week on business connected with Washington College, I found your letter of the 26 Ulto, I regret very much that you never recⁱ my first letter, as you might then perhaps have given me the information I desired, with more ease to yourself, & with more expedition than now. I did not know how to address it, but sent it to a friend in Richmond, who gave it to one of our officers going South, who transferred it to another &, & after travelling many weary miles, has been recently returned to me. I start it again in pursuit of you, though you did not tell me how to address you. I have almost forgotten what it contained; but I hope it will inform you of my purpose in writing a history of the Campaigns in Virginia & of the object that I have in view, so that you may give me all the information in your power. I shall be in no hurry in publishing, & will not do so, until I feel satisfied that

I have got the true story, as my only object is
to disseminate the truth. I am very sorry to
hear that your records were destroyed too, but I
hope Sorrel & Latrobe will be able to supply you
with all you require. I wish to state the acts
of all the Corps of the Army of N. Va: whenever
they did duty, & do not wish to omit so im-
-portant a one as yours. I will therefore wait
as long as I can;

I shall be very glad to receive any thing
you may give to Col. Washington McLean,
as I know you recommend no one but those
who deserve your good opinion.

I am delighted to hear that your arm is still
improving & hope it will soon be restored. You are
however becoming so accomplished with your left
hand, as not to need it. You must remember
me very kindly to Mrs. Longstreet & all your children. I
have not had an opportunity yet to return the Com-
-pliment she paid me. I had while in Richmond
a great many inquiries after you, & learned that you
intended commencing business in New Orleans. If
you become as good a merchant as you were a
soldier I shall be content. No one will then excell
you, & no one can wish you more success & more
happiness than I. My interest & affection for

you will never cease, & my prayers are always
offered for your prosperity —
        I am most truly yours
                                    R E Lee

Strange words from the commander to the subordinate whose disobedience at Gettysburg, according to Rev. Dr. Pendleton and others, led the way to Appomattox.

While General Longstreet held General Lee to be a great strategist, he thought him to be less able as an offensive battle tactician. Those views are shared by many other military officers, who have of late given free expression to them. The Gettysburg controversies, followed by such criticisms, led to the belief that Longstreet was the open enemy of Lee's fame, and lost no opportunity to maliciously decry his military ability. But this is a mistake. General Longstreet's intimate friends know that he has always born for General Lee the most profound love and respect, both as a man and as a commander. His views of Lee's military capacity are discriminating and just, and they are probably correct.

Longstreet saw things military with a practical eye. A fine professional soldier himself, who had taken hard knocks on many great fields, he clearly discerned General Lee's incomparable attributes as a commander, and was never loath to praise them. He also knew Lee's weaknesses, and has sometimes spoken of them, but never in malice or contemptuously. Those who read his utterances in that sense are very narrow indeed. He has never, like the mass of Southerners, looked upon Lee as infallible, yet in one particular Longstreet has held him to be one of the very greatest of commanders.

As an example of General Longstreet's estimate of Lee's professional place in history, one of his interviews when on a visit to the Antietam battlefield, published a few years ago, is quoted:

> General Lee, as a rule, did not underestimate his opponents or the fighting qualities of the Federal troops. But after Chancellorsville he came to have unlimited confidence in his own army, and undoubtedly exaggerated its capacity to overcome obstacles, to march, to fight, to bear up under deprivations and exhaustion. It was a dangerous confidence. I think every officer who served under him will unhesitatingly agree with me on this point.

In answer to a question as to which he regarded as Lee's best battle:

> Well, perhaps the second Battle of Manassas was, all things considered, the best tactical battle General Lee ever fought. The grand strategy of the campaign was also fine, and seems to have completely deceived General Pope. Indeed, Pope failed to com-

prehend Lee's purpose from start to finish. Pope was outgeneralled and outclassed by Lee, and through improper dispositions his fine army was outfought. Still, it will not do to underrate Pope; he was an enterprising soldier and a fighter.

General Longstreet, in the interview at Antietam, summed up Lee's characteristics as a commander in the following succinct manner:

General Lee was a large-minded man, of great and profound learning in the science of war. In all strategical movements he handled a great army with comprehensive ability and signal success. His campaigns against McClellan and Pope fully illustrate his capacity. On the defensive General Lee was absolutely perfect. Reconciled to the single purpose of defence, he was invincible. But of the art of war, more particularly that of giving offensive battle, I do not think General Lee was a master. In science and military learning he was greatly the superior of General Grant, or any other commander on either side. But in the art of war I have no doubt that Grant and several other officers were his equals. In the field his characteristic fault was headlong combativeness.

His impatience to strike, once in the presence of the enemy, whatever the disparity of forces or relative conditions, I consider the one weakness of General Lee's military character. This trait of aggressiveness led him to take too many chances—into dangerous situations. At Gettysburg, all the vast interests at stake and the improbability of success would not deter him. In the immediate presence of the enemy General Lee's mind, at all other times calm and clear, became excited. The same may be said of most other highly educated, theoretical soldiers, General Lee had the absolute confidence of his own troops, and the most unquestioning support of his subordinates. He was wholesomely feared by the Federal rank and file, who undoubtedly considered him the easy superior of their own generals. These were tremendous advantages.

It is very difficult to detect malice or hatred in these calm and dispassionate conclusions.

It is most probable that General Longstreet would have never written or uttered one word concerning Gettysburg had it not been for the attempt of wordy soldiers to specifically fix upon him the whole burden of that battle, their rashness carrying them so far as to lead them to put false orders in the mouth of the great captain, and charge Longstreet with having broken them. To disprove these untrue assertions, and to give the world the truth concerning the battle, then became what General Longstreet considered an imperative duty. He has always regretted deeply that this discussion was not opened before the death of General Lee. If the charges so vehemently urged had been preferred or even suggested in Lee's lifetime, Longstreet does not believe they would have needed any reply from him. General Lee would have answered them himself and set history right.

'The military bill and amendments are the only peace-offerings they have for us, and should be accepted as the starting-point for future issues.

'Like others of the South not previously connected with politics, I naturally acquiesced in the ways of Democracy, but, so far as I can judge, there is nothing tangible in them, beyond the issues that were put to test in the war and there lost. As there is nothing left to take hold of except prejudice, which cannot be worked for good for any one, it seems proper and right that we should seek some standing which may encourage hope for the future.

'If I appreciate the issues of Democracy at this moment, they are the enfranchisement of the negro and the rights of Congress in the premises, but the acts have been passed, are parts of the laws of the land, and no power but Congress can remove them.

'Besides, if we now accept the doctrine that the States only can legislate on suffrage, we will fix the negro vote upon us, for he is now a suffragan, and his vote, with the vote that will go with him, will hold to his rights, while, by recognising the acts of Congress, we may, after a fair trial, if negro suffrage proves a mistake, appeal and have Congress correct the error. It will accord better with wise policy to insist that the negro shall vote in the Northern as well as the Southern States.

'If everyone will meet the crisis with proper appreciation of our condition and obligations, the sun will rise tomorrow on a happy people. Our fields will again begin to yield their increase, our railways and water will teem with abundant commerce, our towns and cities will resound with the tumult of trader and we will be reinvigorated by the blessings of Almighty God.

'Very respectfully yours,

'James Longstreet.'

I might have added that not less forceful than the grounds I gave were the obligations under which we were placed by the terms of our paroles,—'To respect the laws of Congress,'—but the letter was enough.

The afternoon of the day upon which my letter was published the paper that had called for advice published a column of editorial calling me traitor! deserter of my friends! and accusing me of joining the enemy! but did not publish a line of the letter upon which it based the charges! Other papers of the Democracy took up the garbled representation of this journal and spread it broadcast, not even giving the letter upon which they based their evil attacks upon me.

Up to that time the First Corps, in all oi its parts, in all of its history, was above reproach. I was in successful business in New Orleans as cotton factor, with a salary from an insurance company of five thousand dollars per year.

The day after the announcement old comrades passed me on the streets without speaking. Business began to grow dull, General Hood (the only one of my old comrades who occasionally visited me) thought that he could save the insurance business, and in a few weeks I found myself at leisure.

Two years after that period, on March 4, 1869, General Grant was inaugurated President of the United States, and in the bigness of his generous heart called me to Washington. Before I found opportunity to see him he sent my name to the Senate for confirmation as surveyor of customs at New Orleans. I was duly confirmed, and held the office until 1878, when I resigned. Since that time, I have lived in New Orleans, Louisiana, and in Gainesville, Georgia, surrounded by a few of my old friends, and in occasional appreciative touch with others, South and North.

Lee's Right Wing at Gettysburg

By James Longstreet

Gettysburg lies partly between Seminary Ridge on the west and Cemetery Ridge on the south-east, a distance of about fourteen hundred yards dividing the crests of the two ridges. As General Lee rode to the summit of Seminary Ridge and looked down upon the town he saw the Federals in full retreat and concentrating on the rock-ribbed hill that served as a burying-ground for the city. He sent orders to Ewell to follow up the success if he found it practicable and to occupy the hill on which the enemy was concentrating. As the order was not positive, but left discretion with General Ewell, the latter thought it better to give his troops a little rest and wait for more definite instructions. I was following Hill's Corps as fast as possible, and as soon as I got possession of the road went rapidly forward to join General Lee. I found him on the summit of Seminary Ridge watching the enemy concentrate on the opposite hill. He pointed out their position to me. I took my glasses and made as careful a survey as I could from that point. After five or ten minutes, I turned to General Lee and said:

"If we could have chosen a point to meet our plans of operation, I do not think we could have found a better one than that upon which

THE LAST CONFEDERATE GUN AT GETTYSBURG—ON LONGSTREET'S RIGHT, OPPOSITE ROUND TOP

147

they are now concentrating. All we have to do is to throw our army around by their left, and we shall interpose between the Federal Army and Washington. We can get a strong position and wait, and if they fail to attack us we shall have everything in condition to move back tomorrow night in the direction of Washington, selecting beforehand a good position into which we can place our troops to receive battle next day. Finding our object is Washington or that army, the Federals will be sure to attack us. When they attack, we shall beat them, as we proposed to do before we left Fredericksburg, and the probabilities are that the fruits of our success will be great."

"No," said General Lee; "the enemy is there, and I am going to attack him there."

I suggested that such a move as I proposed would give us control of the roads leading to Washington and Baltimore, and reminded General Lee of our original plans. If we had fallen behind Meade and had insisted on staying between him and Washington, he would have been compelled to attack and would have been badly beaten.

LUTHERAN CHURCH ON CHAMBERSBURG
STREET, GETTYSBURG, USED AS A HOSPITAL.

General Lee answered, "No; they are there in position, and I am going to whip them or they are going to whip me."

I saw he was in no frame of mind to listen to further argument at that time, so I did not push the matter, but determined to renew the subject the next morning. It was then about 5 o'clock in the afternoon. On the morning of the 2nd I joined General Lee and again proposed the move to Meade's left and rear. He was still unwilling to consider the proposition, but soon left me and rode off to see General Ewell and to examine the ground on our left with a view to making the attack at that point. After making the examination and talking to General Ewell, he determined to make the attack by the right, and, returning to where I was, announced his intention of so doing. His engineer officers had been along the line far enough to find a road by which the troops could move and be concealed from the Federal signal stations.

About 11 o'clock on the morning of the 2nd he ordered the march, and put it under the conduct of his engineer officers, so as to be assured that the troops would move by the best route and encounter the least delay in reaching the position designated by him for the attack on the Federal left, at the same time concealing the movements then under orders from view of the Federals.

McLaws's division was in advance, with Hood following. After marching some distance there was a delay in front, and I rode forward to ascertain the cause, when it was reported to me that part of the road just in advance of us was in plain view of the Federal signal station on Round Top. To avoid that point the direction of the troops was changed. Again, I found there was some delay, and ordering Hood's division, then in the rear, to move on and double with the division in front, so as to save as much time as possible, I went forward again to see the cause of the delay. It seemed there was doubt again about the men being concealed, when I stated that I could see the signal station, and there was no reason why they could not see us.

It seemed to me useless, therefore, to delay the troops any longer with the idea of concealing the movement, and the two divisions advanced. As the line was deployed I rode along from left to right, examining the Federal position and putting my troops in the best position we could find. General Lee at the same time gave orders for the attack to be made by my right—following up the direction of the Emmitsburg road toward the Cemetery Ridge, holding Hood's left as well as could be toward the Emmitsburg road, McLaws to follow

BRIGADIER-GENERAL PAUL SEMMES,
C. S. A. MORTALLY WOUNDED, JULY 2

BRIGADIER-GENERAL WILLIAM BARKSDALE,
C. S. A. WOUNDED JULY 2, DIED JULY 3.

the movements of Hood, attacking at the Peach Orchard the Federal Third Corps, with a part of R. H. Anderson's division following the movements of McLaws to guard his left flank.

As soon as the troops were in position, and we could find the points against which we should march and give the guiding points, the advance was ordered—at half-past 3 o'clock in the afternoon. The attack was made in splendid style by both divisions, and the Federal line was broken by the first impact. They retired, many of them, in the direction of Round Top behind bowlders and fences, which gave them shelter, and where they received reinforcements.

This was an unequal battle. General Lee's orders had been that when my advance was made, the Second Corps (Ewell), on his left, should move and make a simultaneous attack; that the Third Corps (Hill) should watch closely and engage so as to prevent heavy massing in front of me. Ewell made no move at all until about 8 o'clock at night, after the heat of the battle was over, his line having been broken by a call for one of his brigades to go elsewhere. Hill made no move whatever, save of the brigades of his right division that were covering our left.

When the battle of the 2nd was over, General Lee pronounced it a success, as we were in possession of ground from which we had driven the Federals and had taken several field-pieces. The conflict had been fierce and bloody, and my troops had driven back heavy columns and had encountered a force three or four times their number, but we had accomplished little toward victorious results. (General Meade's report shows that all of the Third and parts of the Second, Fifth. Sixth, and Twelfth corps were engaged in the second day's fight—Original Editors).

Our success of the first day had led us into battle on the 2nd, and the battle on the 2nd was to lead us into the terrible and hopeless slaughter on the 3rd.

On the night of the 2nd I sent to our extreme right to make a little reconnaissance in that direction, thinking General Lee might yet conclude to move around the Federal left. The morning of the 3rd broke clear and indicated a day on which operations would not be interrupted by the elements. The Confederate forces still occupied Seminary Ridge, while the Federals occupied the range stretching from Round Top to Cemetery Hill and around Culp's Hill. The position of the Federals was quite strong, and the battle of the 2nd had concentrated them so that I considered an attack from the front more

DEAD IN THE "WHEATFIELD" GATHERED FOR BURIAL.
FROM PHOTOGRAPHS.

hazardous than the battle on the 2nd had been. The Federals were concentrated, while our troops were stretched out in a long, broken—and thus a weak—line.

However, General Lee hoped to break through the Federal line and drive them off. I was disappointed when he came to me on the morning of the 3rd and directed that I should renew the attack against Cemetery Hill, probably the strongest point of the Federal line. For that purpose he had already ordered up Pickett's division, which had been left at Chambersburg to guard our supply trains. In the meantime, the Federals had placed batteries on Round Top, in position to make a raking fire against troops attacking the Federal front. Meade knew that if the battle was renewed it would be virtually over the same ground as my battle of the 2nd. I stated to General Lee that I had been examining the ground over to the right, and was much inclined to think the best thing was to move to the Federal left.

"No," he said; "I am going to take them where they are on Cemetery Hill. I want you to take Pickett's division and make the attack. I will re-enforce you by two divisions (Heth's under Pettigrew and Pender's under Trimble) of the Third Corps."

"That will give me fifteen thousand men," I replied. "I have been a soldier, I may say, from the ranks up to the position I now hold. I have been in pretty much all kinds of skirmishes, from those of two or three soldiers up to those of an army corps, and I think I can safely say there never was a body of fifteen thousand men who could make that attack successfully."

The general seemed a little impatient at my remarks, so I said nothing more. As he showed no indication of changing his plan, I went to work at once to arrange my troops for the attack. Pickett was put in position and received directions for the line of his advance as indicated by General Lee. The divisions of the Third Corps were arranged along his left with orders to take up the line of march, as Pickett passed before them, in short echelon. We were to open with our batteries, and Pickett was to move out as soon as we silenced the Federal batteries. The artillery combat was to begin with the rapid discharge of two field-pieces as our signal.

As soon as the orders were communicated along the line, I sent Colonel E. P. Alexander (who was commanding a battalion of artillery and who had been an engineer officer) to select carefully a point from which he could observe the effect of our batteries. When he could discover the enemy's batteries silenced or crippled, he should give no-

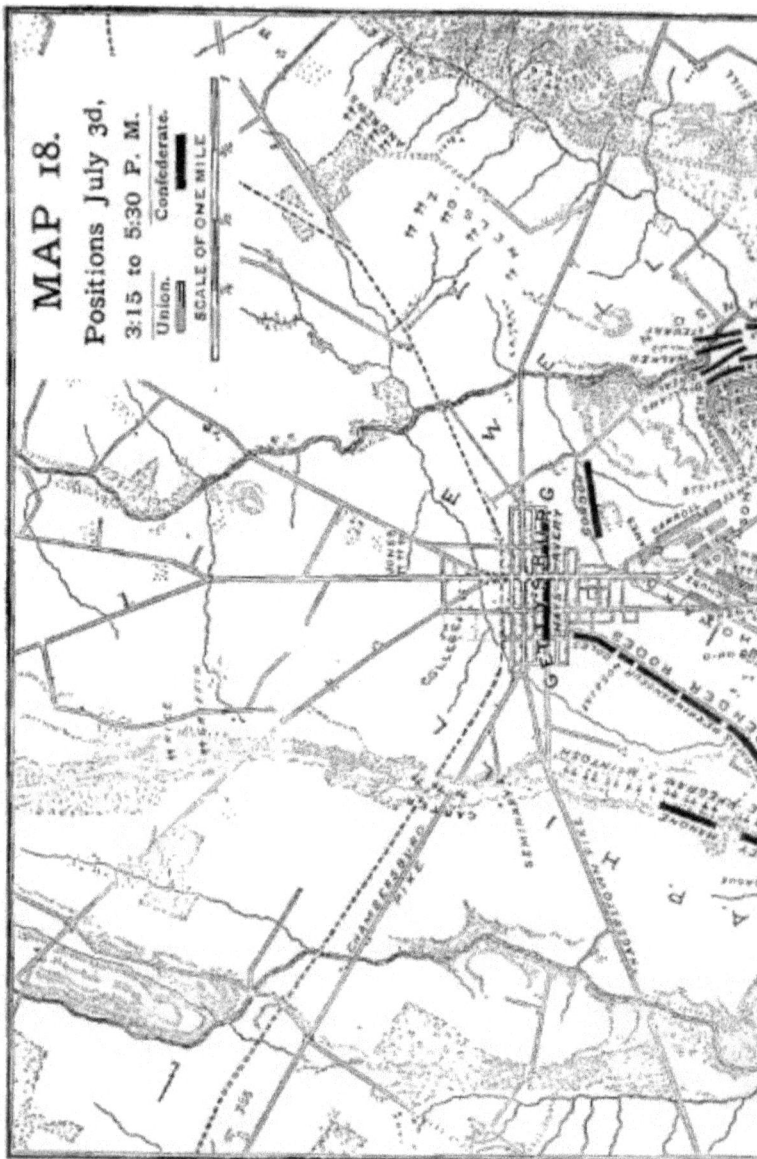

MAP 18.
Positions July 3d,
3:15 to 5:30 P. M.

Union. Confederate.

SCALE OF ONE MILE

tice to General Pickett, who was ordered, upon receipt of that notice, to move forward to the attack.

When I took Pickett to the crest of Seminary Ridge and explained where his troops should be sheltered, and pointed out the direction General Lee wished him to take and the point of the Federal line where the assault was to be made, he seemed to appreciate the severity of the contest upon which he was about to enter, but was quite hopeful of success. Upon receipt of notice, he was to march over the crest of the hill down the gentle slope and up the rise opposite the Federal stronghold. The distance was about fourteen hundred yards, and for most of the way the Federal batteries would have a raking fire from Round Top, while the sharpshooters, artillery, and infantry would subject the assaulting column to a terrible and destructive fire.

With my knowledge of the situation, I could see the desperate and hopeless nature of the charge and the cruel slaughter it would cause. My heart was heavy when I left Pickett. I rode once or twice along the ground between Pickett and the Federals, examining the positions and studying the matter over in all its phases so far as we could anticipate.

About 1 o'clock everything was in readiness. The signal guns broke the prevailing stillness, and immediately 150 Confederate cannon burst into a deafening roar, which was answered by a thunder almost as great from the Federal side. The great artillery combat proceeded. The destruction was, of course, not great; but the thunder on Seminary Ridge, and the echo from the Federal side, showed that both commanders were ready. The armies seemed like mighty wild beasts growling at each other and preparing for a death struggle. For an hour or two the fire was continued, and met such steady response on the part of the Federals, that it seemed less effective than we had anticipated.

I sent word to Alexander that unless he could do something more, I would not feel warranted in ordering the troops forward. After a little, some of the Federal batteries ceased firing, possibly to save ammunition, and Alexander thought the most suitable time for the advance had come. He sent word to Pickett, and Pickett rode to my headquarters.

As he came up he asked if the time for his advance had come. I was convinced that he would be leading his troops to needless slaughter, and did not speak. He repeated the question, and without opening my lips I bowed in answer. In a determined voice Pickett said: "Sir, I shall lead my division forward." He then remounted his horse and rode back to his command. I mounted my horse and rode to a point where I could observe the troops as they marched forward. Colonel Alexander had set aside a battery of seven guns to advance with Pickett, but General Pendleton, from whom they were borrowed, recalled them just before the charge was ordered. Colonel Alexander told me of the seven guns which had been removed, and that his ammunition was so low he could not properly support the charge. I ordered him to stop Pickett until the ammunition could be replenished, and he answered, "There is no ammunition with which to replenish." In the hurry, he got together such guns as he could to move with Pickett.

It has been said that I should have exercised discretion and should not have sent Pickett on his charge. It has been urged that I had exercised discretion on previous occasions. It is true that at times when I saw a certainty of success in another direction, I did not follow the orders of my general, but that was when he was not near and could not see the situation as it existed. When your chief is away, you have a right to exercise discretion; but if he sees everything that you see, you have no right to disregard his positive and repeated orders. I never exercised discretion after discussing with General Lee the points of his orders, and when, after discussion, he had ordered the execution of his policy. I had offered my objections to Pickett's battle and had been over ruled, and I was in the immediate presence of the commanding general when the order was given for Pickett to advance.

That day at Gettysburg was one of the saddest of my life. I foresaw what my men would meet and would gladly have given up my position rather than share in the responsibilities of that day. It was thus I felt when Pickett at the head of 4900 brave men marched over the crest of Seminary Ridge and began his descent of the slope. As he passed me he rode gracefully, with his jaunty cap raked well over on his right ear and his long auburn locks, nicely dressed, hanging almost to his shoulders. He seemed rather a holiday soldier than a general at the head of a column which was about to make one of the grandest, most desperate assaults recorded in the annals of wars.

Armistead and Garnett, two of his brigadiers, were veterans of nearly a quarter of a century's service. Their minds seemed absorbed in the men behind, and in the bloody work before them. Kemper, the other brigadier, was younger but had experienced many severe battles. He was leading my old brigade that I had drilled on Manassas plains before the first battle on that noted field. The troops advanced in well-

CEMETERY HILL.   CLUMP OF TREES.   ROUND TOP.

PROFILE OF CEMETERY RIDGE AS SEEN FROM PICKETT'S POSITION BEFORE THE CHARGE.

closed ranks and with elastic step, their faces lighted with hope. Before them lay the ground over which they were to pass to the point of attack. Intervening were several fences, a field of corn, a little swale running through it and then a rise from that point to the Federal stronghold.

As soon as Pickett passed the crest of the hill, the Federals had a clear view and opened their batteries, and as he descended the eastern slope of the ridge his troops received a fearful fire from the batteries in front and from Round Top. The troops marched steadily, taking the fire with great coolness. As soon as they passed my batteries I ordered my artillery to turn their fire against the batteries on our right then raking my lines. They did so, but did not force the Federals to change the direction of their fire and relieve our infantry. As the troops were about to cross the swale I noticed a considerable force of Federal infantry moving down as though to flank the left of our line. I sent an officer to caution the division commanders to guard against that move, at the same time sending another staff-officer with similar orders so as to feel assured the order would be delivered. Both officers came back bringing their saddles, their horses having been shot under them.

After crossing the swale, the troops kept the same steady step, but met a dreadful fire at the hands of the Federal sharpshooters; and as soon as the field was open the Federal infantry poured down a terrific fire which was kept up during the entire assault. The slaughter was terrible, the enfilade fire of the batteries on Round Top being very destructive. At times one shell would knock down five or six men. I dismounted to relieve my horse and was sitting on a rail fence watching very closely the movements of the troops. Colonel Fremantle, who had taken a position behind the Third Corps where he would be out of reach of fire and at the same time have a clear view of the field, became so interested that he left his position and came with speed to join me.

Just as he came up behind me, Pickett had reached a point near the Federal lines. A pause was made to close ranks and mass for the final plunge. The troops on Pickett's left, although advancing, were evidently a little shaky. Colonel Fremantle, only observing the troops of Pickett's command, said to me, "General, I would not have missed this for anything in the world." He believed it to be a complete success. I was watching the troops supporting Pickett and saw plainly they could not hold together ten minutes longer. I called his attention to

MAJOR-GENERAL WILLIAM D. PENDER,
WOUNDED JULY 2, DIED JULY 18.

BRIGADIER-GENERAL LEWIS A. ARMI-
STEAD, C.S. A., KILLED JULY 3.

the wavering condition of the two divisions of the Third Corps, and said they would not hold, that Pickett would strike and be crushed and the attack would be a failure. As Pickett's division concentrated in making the final assault, Kemper fell severely wounded.

As the division threw itself against the Federal line Garnett fell and expired. The Confederate flag was planted in the Federal line, and immediately Armistead fell mortally wounded at the feet of the Federal soldiers. The wavering divisions then seemed appalled, broke their ranks, and retired. Immediately the Federals swarmed around Pickett, attacking on all sides, enveloped and broke up his command, having killed and wounded more than two thousand men in about thirty minutes. They then drove the fragments back upon our lines. As they came back I fully expected to see Meade ride to the front and lead his forces to a tremendous counter-charge.

Sending my staff-officers to assist in collecting the fragments of my command, I rode to my line of batteries, knowing they were all I had in front of the impending attack, resolved to drive it back or sacrifice my last gun and man. The Federals were advancing a line of skirmishers which I thought was the advance of their charge. As soon as the line of skirmishers came within reach of our guns, the batteries opened again and their fire seemed to check at once the threatened advance. After keeping it up a few minutes the line of skirmishers disappeared, and my mind was relieved of the apprehension that Meade was going to follow us.

General Lee came up as our troops were falling back and encouraged them as well as he could; begged them to re-form their ranks and reorganise their forces, and assisted the staff-officers in bringing them all together again. It was then he used the expression that has been mentioned so often:

> It was all my fault; get together, and let us do the best we can toward saving that which is left us.

As our troops were driven back from the general assault an attack was made on my extreme right by several squadrons of cavalry, which succeeded in breaking through our line of pickets. They were met by a counter-move of the 9th Georgia and the well-directed fire of Captain Bachman's battery and driven back, the 11th and 59th Georgia joining in the countermove.

Finding that Meade was not going to follow us, I prepared to withdraw my line to a better defensive position. The batteries were withdrawn well over Seminary Ridge, and orders were sent to the right for McLaws's and Hood's divisions to be withdrawn to corresponding positions. The armies remained in position, the Confederates on Seminary Ridge extending around Gettysburg, the left also drawn back, the Federals on Cemetery Ridge, until the night of the 4th, when we took up the march in retreat for Virginia.

That night, while we were standing round a little fire by the roadside, General Lee said again the defeat was all his fault. He said to me at another time, "You ought not to have made that last attack."

I replied, "I had my orders, and they were of such a nature there was no escape from them."

During that winter, while I was in east Tennessee, in a letter I received from him he said:

> If I only had taken your counsel even on the 3rd, and had moved around the Federal left, how different all might have been.

The only thing Pickett said of his charge was that he was distressed at the loss of his command. He thought he should have had two of his brigades that had been left in Virginia; with them he felt that he would have broken the line.

While I was trying to persuade General Lee to turn the Federal left on the 1st of July, Halleck telegraphed Meade as follows:

> Washington, D. C., July 1st, 1863.
> The movements of the enemy yesterday indicate his intention to either turn your left, or to cover himself by the South Mountain and occupy Cumberland Valley. Do not let him draw you too far to the east.

Again, on the same day:

> ... Your tactical arrangements for battle seem good, so far as I can judge from my knowledge of the character of the country; but in a strategic view, are you not too far east, arid may not Lee attempt to turn your left and cut you off from Frederick? Please give your full attention to this suggestion. . . .

The next day, just thirty minutes before my assault, General Meade telegraphed General Halleck at 3 p. m:

> ... If I find it hazardous to do so (meaning to attack), or am satisfied that the enemy is endeavouring to move to my rear

and interpose between me and Washington, I shall fall back to my supplies at Westminster. . . .

From this we know that the ground of the Gettysburg cemetery could have been occupied without the loss of a man, yet even at this late day, some of the Virginians, not satisfied with the sacrifice already made, wish that I, who would and could have saved every man lost at Gettysburg, should now be shot to death.

If we had made the move around the Federal left, and taken a strong position, we should have dislodged Meade without a single blow; but even if we had been successful at Gettysburg, and had driven the Federals out of their stronghold, we should have won a fruitless victory, and returned to Virginia conquered victors. The ground they occupied would have been worth no more to us than the ground we were on. What we needed was a battle that would give us decided fruits, not ground that was of no value. I do not think there was any necessity for giving battle at Gettysburg.

All of our cavalry was absent, and while that has been urged by some as a reason why the battle should have been made at once, to my mind it was one of the strongest reasons for delaying the battle until everything was well in hand. The cause of the battle was simply General Lee's determination to fight it out from the position in which he was at that time. He did not feel that he was beaten on the second day, but that he was the victor, and still hoped he would be able to dislodge Meade; but he made a mistake in sending such a small number of men to attack a formidable force in a position of great natural strength, re-enforced by such temporary shelter as could be collected and placed in position to cover the troops. Lee's hope in entering the campaign was that he would be in time to make a successful battle north of the Potomac, with such advantages as to draw off the army at Vicksburg as well as the Federal troops at other points.

I do not think the general effect of the battle was demoralising, but by a singular coincidence our army at Vicksburg surrendered to Grant on the 4th, while the armies of Lee and Meade were lying in front of each other, each waiting a movement on the part of the other, neither victor, neither vanquished. This surrender, taken in connection with the Gettysburg defeat, was, of course, very discouraging to our superior officers, though I do not know that it was felt as keenly by the rank and file. For myself, I felt that our last hope was gone, and that it was now only a question of time with us.

MAJOR-GENERAL GEORGE E. PICKETT, C. S. A.

When, however, I found that Rosecrans was moving down toward Georgia against General Bragg, I thought it possible we might recover some of our lost prospects by concentrating against Rosecrans, destroying his army, and advancing through Kentucky. General Lee evidently felt severely mortified and hurt at the failure, so much so that at times he was inclined to listen to some of those who claimed to be his friends, and to accept their proposition to find a scapegoat. He resisted them, however, and seemed determined to leave the responsibility on his own hands.

For several reasons, I will take occasion here to answer some serious charges that have been made against me by men who claim to have been the friends of General Lee.

Mr. Jefferson Davis, in his *Rise and Fall of the Confederate Government* (Vol. II.), quotes from a memorial address the old story of the Rev. W. N. Pendleton:

The ground south-west of the town was carefully examined by me after the engagement on July 1st. Being found much less difficult than the steep ascent fronting the troops already up, its practicable character was reported to our commanding general.

He informed me that he had ordered Longstreet to attack on that front at sunrise the next morning. And he added to myself, I want you to be out long before sunrise, so as to re-examine and save time.

He also desired me to communicate with General Longstreet us well as with himself. The reconnaissance was accordingly made as soon as it was light enough on the 2nd, and made through a long distance—in fact, very close to what there was of the enemy's line. No insuperable difficulty appearing, and the marching up—far off, the enemy's re-enforcing columns being seen, the extreme desirableness of immediate attack there was at once reported to the commanding general; and, according to his wish, message was also sent to the intrepid but deliberate corps commander, whose sunrise attack there had been ordered. There was, however, unaccountable delay.

My own messages went repeatedly to General Lee, and his I know was urgently pressed on General Longstreet until, as I afterward learned from officers who saw General Lee—as I could not at the time—he manifested extreme displeasure with the tardy corps commander. That hard-fighting soldier, to whom it had been committed there to attack early in the day, did not in person reach the commanding general and with him ride to a position whence to view the ground and see the enemy's arriving masses, until 12 o'clock, and his column was not up and ready for the assault until 4 p. m. All this, as it occurred under my personal observation, it is nothing short of imperative duty that I should thus fairly state.

Mr. Davis indorses the statement thus:

For the reasons set forth by General Pendleton, whose statement in regard to a fact coming under his personal observation none who knew him will question, preparations for a general engagement were unfortunately delayed until the afternoon instead of being made at sunrise; then troops had been concentrated, and Round Top. the commanding position unoccupied in the morning, had received the force which inflicted such disaster on our assaulting columns. The question as to the responsibility for this delay has been so fully discussed in the *Southern Historical Society Papers* as to relieve me from the necessity of entering into it.

As General Pendleton's lecture was the capital upon which it was proposed to draw funds for a memorial church, it was natural, perhaps, that Mr. Davis should, *as a sentiment*, claim the statements made as beyond question. Most Virginia writers on this subject have taken up and followed the false scent announced by General Pendleton. Outside that State, I believe Mr. Davis and General Wilcox are the only persons who do not spurn it as false. Facts connected with this battle have been so distorted and misrepresented that a volume of distinct maps must be written in order to make a demonstration, to the letter, of all its features.

General C. M. Wilcox, in an article in the number of the *Southern Historical Society Papers* for September, 1877, refers to the order for early attack, *viz*.:

> It has been asserted that General Longstreet was ordered to attack at daylight or early the next morning. Of this I have no knowledge personally, but am inclined to believe that he was so ordered.

But from the *official accounts* of Generals Pendleton and Wilcox (*Official Records*, Vol. XXVIL, Part II.,) we see that the right of General Lee's army was not deployed as far as the Fairfield road on the 1st of July, that General Pendleton did not pass beyond this road, and only noted the location of the ridge on the right from his position on the Fairfield road especially as likely to be important "toward a flank movement." With this idea in his mind lie leaves us to infer that he left our right and moved over to our left to supervise the posting of artillery battalions just then coming up.

Soon after General Pendleton passed from about the Fairfield road to our left, the division of General R. H. Anderson,—of the Third Corps,—led by the brigade of General C. M. Wilcox, filed off to the right from the Chambersburg road, marched in an oblique direction toward the Fairfield road, where it was halted for the night, lying in bivouac, till the next day, the brigade of Wilcox being on picket or guard service during the night about a mile farther to the right. In the absence of other evidence, one might be at a loss to know which of these accounts was intended in a Pickwickian sense, but the account of General R. H. Anderson, who was guileless and truthful, supports the official reports.

General A. A. Humphreys (of the other side), late chief of the United States Corps of Engineers, a man whose entire life and service were devoted to official accuracy, gives similar evidence in his official report. (*Official Records*, Vol. XXVII., Part 1).

All the subordinate reports on the Confederate side confirm the account by General Anderson, while the reports of subordinate officers on the Federal side conform to that of General Humphreys. It is conclusive therefore that the Confederates occupied no ground east of the Fairfield road till R. H. Anderson's division advanced on the morning of the 2nd at 10 to find its position on the right of Hill's corps, after a clever fight between the 3rd Maine and 1st U. S. Sharpshooters against the 10th and 11th Alabama regiments.

When it is remembered that my command was at the close of the first day's fight fifteen to twenty miles west of the field, that its attack as ordered was to be made along the east side of the Emmitsburg road, that no part of General Lee's army touched that road till 9 a. m. of the 2nd, that up to that hour it was in possession of the Federals, and that their troops had been marching in by that road from early on the 1st till 8 a. m. on the 2nd, it will be seen that General Pendleton's reconnaissance on the 1st was made, if made at all, by his passing through the Federal lines on the afternoon of the 1st and again on the morning of the 2nd.

General Wilcox confesses want of personal information of the order for daylight or early attack, but expresses his confidence that the order was given. That is, he, occupying our extreme right on the 1st, on picket at a point considerably west of the Emmitsburg road, believes that General Lee ordered troops some fifteen or twenty miles off, and yet on the march, to pass his picket guard in the night to the point of attack, east of the Emmitsburg road, through the Federal lines, in order to make a daylight attack east of the road. While I am prepared to admit that General Lee ordered, at times, desperate battles, I cannot admit that he, blindfold, ever led or ordered his next in rank, also blindfold, into night marches through the enemy's lines to gain position and make a battle at daylight next morning.

In articles formerly published on this charge of General Pendleton, masses of evidence were adduced showing that my column when ordered to the right, east of the Emmitsburg road, was conducted by General Lee's engineer officer; that when halted under the conduct of that officer I doubled the rear division on the leading one so as to save time; that my arrangements were promptly made, and that my attack was made many hours before any of our other troops were ready to obey their orders to cooperate. As I was the only one prepared for battle, I contended against the Federal army throughout the contest with two divisions and some misguided brigades sent to cover my left.

Colonel Taylor, of General Lee's staff, takes exception to the delay in the attack of Pickett on the last day under the impression that, had I attacked earlier and before Edward Johnson was driven from the Federal right, the latter might have held his ground longer and to some advantage to the Confederates. He seems to lose sight of the fact that General Lee, not I, was commanding our left under Johnson, and that he alone could order concert of action. On the 2nd, notwithstanding his orders to move in concert with my attack at 4 p. m., Johnson did not go in till 8 at night, long after my battle was ended. Colonel Taylor thinks the forlorn-hope should have gone in sooner. The universal opinion now is that it should not have gone in at all; and, as already stated, that was the opinion General Lee expressed soon after the battle.

Some of our North Carolina troops seem to consider the less conspicuous part given them a reflection upon them as soldiers of true mettle and dash. This sensitiveness is not well founded. Every officer of experience knows that the best of veteran soldiers, with bloody noses from a fresh battle, are never equal to those going in fresh in their first stroke of the battle. Had Pickett's men gone through the same experience as the other troops on the 1st, they could not have felt the same zest for fighting that they did coming up fresh and feeling disparaged that the army had won new laurels in their absence. There is no doubt that the North Carolinians did as well as any soldiers could have done under the circumstances. I can truthfully attest that the old North State furnished as fine and gallant troops as any that fought in the Confederate ranks—and that is saying as much as can be said for soldiers. They certainly made sufficient sacrifice, and that was all we had left to do on that day.

During the Franco-Prussian war I kept a map of the field of operations with coloured pegs, that were moved from day to day to indicate the movements of the two armies. Bazaine had been driven to shelter at Metz, McMahon had been driven back to the route leading from Paris to Metz and seemed in doubt whether he would go to Paris or to Bazaine's relief. He suffered himself to be forced north of the route between these points. On the morning that the wires brought us that information, two or three of the French Creoles of New Orleans visited my office to ask my views of the movements then proceeding.

I replied, "McMahon's army will be prisoners of war in ten days."

They were very indignant and stated that I was a Republican and in sympathy with the Prussians. My reply was that I had only given them my solution of a military problem. The Prussians were on the shorter route to Paris or to Metz, so that if McMahon should attempt to move in either direction the Prussians, availing themselves of the shorter lines, would interpose and force McMahon to attack; but as he had already been so beaten and demoralised, that he could not be expected to make a successful attack and would therefore be obliged to surrender. If he had gone direct to Paris before giving up his shorter route, it is possible that he could have organised a succouring army for the relief of Metz.

Had we interposed between Meade and Washington our army in almost as successful prestige as was that of the Prussians, Meade would have been obliged to attack us wherever we might be pleased to have him. He would have been badly beaten like the French, and the result would have been similar. I do not mean to say that two governments would have been permanently established; for I thought before the war, and during its continuance, that the people would eventually get together again in stronger bonds of friendship than those of their first love.

The Charge of Pickett, Pettigrew, and Trimble
By J. B. Smith.
(From the *Bivouac* of March, 1887, and editorially revised.—Original Editors).

In an address delivered by Colonel Andrew Cowan to his comrades at Gettysburg on the 3rd of July, 1886, he, like nearly every other speaker and writer, ascribes all the praise of the Confederate charge of the third day to Pickett's division. He says: "Beyond the wall nothing but the grey-clad Virginians." He speaks of no other troops except Pickett's. Some writers have gone so far as to say Pickett made the immortal charge with five thousand Virginians, etc. Pickett's division was fresh, not having engaged the enemy on the first or second day, while the other troops of the assaulting body fought on the previous days with un surpassed bravery, and some of the brigades were almost annihilated.

The grand assaulting column was formed in three divisions, and the divisions were commanded and led to the slaughter by Pickett, Pettigrew, and Trimble.

General George E. Pickett's division, composed of three brigades

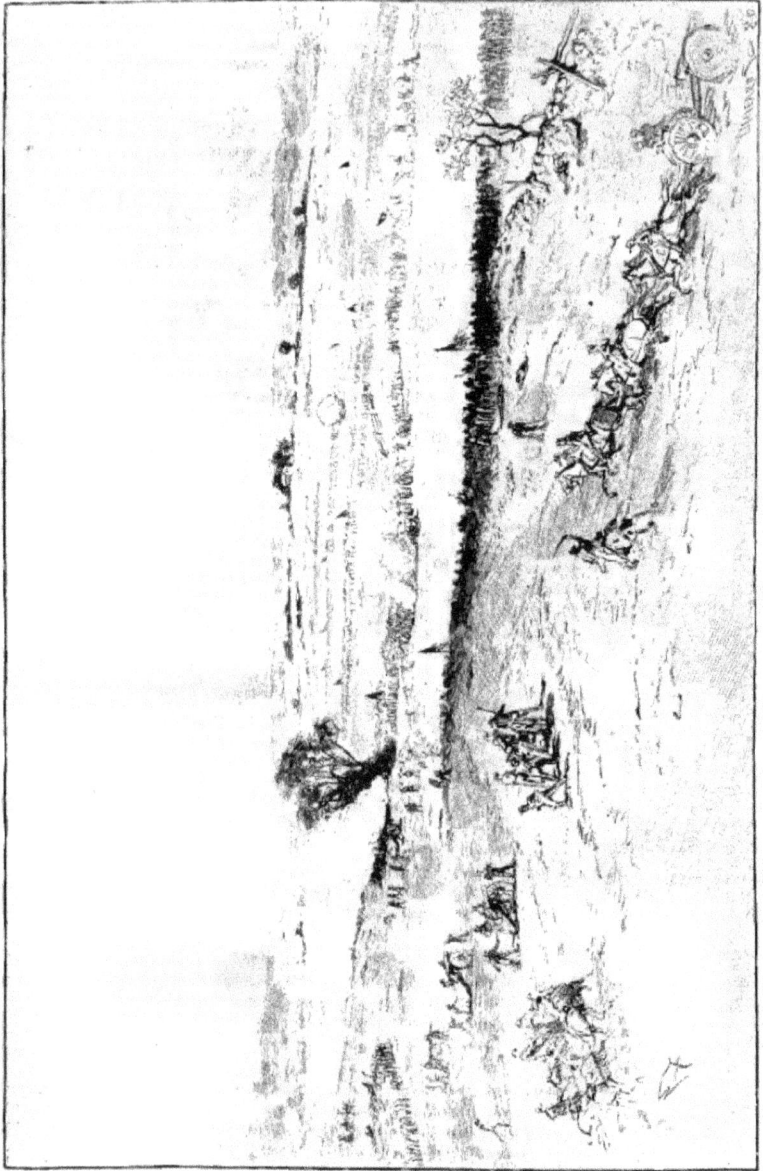

THE CHARGE OF PICKETT, PETTIGREW, & TRIMBLE. FROM A WARTIME SKETCH FROM THE UNION POSITION

commanded by Generals Richard B. Garnett, Lewis A. Armistead, and James L. Kemper, was 4900 strong. Garnett fell during the progress of the charge while at the head of his column urging his men on. Armistead led his men through the terrific storm of battle to the base of the Federal works, and there he placed his cap on his sword and scaled the wall, appealing to his troops to follow him. A few of his disorganised men imitated his heroic example, and died at his feet. General Kemper was wounded in the charge.

General J. Johnston Pettigrew's command embraced the following brigades: Archer's Tennessee brigade, commanded by Colonel Fry, of the 13th Alabama; Pettigrew's North Carolina brigade, Jo Davis's Mississippi brigade, and Brockenbrough's brigade of Virginians, aggregating five thousand troops. All were of Heth's division of A. P. Hill's corps. General Pettigrew was wounded in the charge, but he did not quit the field, and remained in command until he fell at Falling Waters.

I will now notice the conduct of Archer's Tennessee brigade. It opened the battle on the first day and lost its brave and gallant commander. While leading his men he was captured by a flank movement made by the enemy. The brigade suffered heavy losses in other ways on that day. When the grand assault was made on the 3rd, the 1st and 7th Tennessee regiments made the first breach in the Federal works on Cemetery Hill, and they were the only organised regiments that entered into and beyond the enemy's walls.

The 14th Tennessee, after losing heavily on the first day, went into the grand charge with 375 men, and planted its colours on the stone wall and left them there. The heroic conduct of the 13th Alabama in that awful and trying scene has been carefully written up, and the record is in the archives of the Southern Historical Society, in its native State, and will be loved and admired as long as heroism is admired. It was Archer's worn, tattered, and bleeding brigade that fought the last battle north of the Potomac—the Battle of Falling Waters—where the lamented Pettigrew fell.

Davis's Mississippi brigade, that fought so gallantly on the first day, and crossed bayonets with the Iron Brigade, had a prominent part in the grand charge. The 2nd Mississippi of that brigade lost half of its men on that day, but was still intact, ready and willing to fight, and its courage in the great charge has become a matter of history. Its battle-flag is in the possession of the old colour-bearer, who lives, (at time of publication) at Blossom Prairie, Texas, and has the names of more than a score of battles stamped on it.

Scales sand Lane's North Carolina brigades, commanded by General Isaac K. Trimble, belonged to General W. D. Pender's division of A. P. Hill's corps, and were 2500 strong. General Fender was mortally wounded on the second day. When General Lee saw the men of Scales's brigade, bleeding from wounds received on the first day, he said, "Many of these poor fellows should go to the rear." When a brigade would fight under such circumstances as Scales's did, it ought not to be robbed of its military fame. General Trimble was wounded in the charge.

Prairie Grove, Tex.

A Reply to General Longstreet.
By William Allan, Lieutenant-Colonel, C. S. A.

General Longstreet's account of Gettysburg is notable for its mistakes as well as for its attitude toward General Lee and others.

First. The statement that General Lee passed over more deserving officers from other States in order to give the command of his corps to Virginians is an unworthy attack upon a man who was as singularly free from such prejudices as he was from self-seeking, either during the war or after it. Lee said in a letter to President Davis, October 2nd, 1862, at the close of the Antietam campaign:

> In reference to commanders of corps with the rank of lieutenant-general, of which you request my opinion, I can confidently recommend Generals Longstreet and Jackson, in this army. My opinion of the merits of General Jackson has been greatly enhanced during this expedition. He is true, honest, and brave; has a single eye to the good of the service, and spares no exertion to accomplish his object. Next to these two officers I consider General A. P. Hill the best commander with me. He fights his troops well and takes good care of them. At present, I do not think that more than two commanders of corps are necessary for this army.

This was Lee's judgment after a campaign in which both the Hills and McLaws had served, and long before there was any question of making either of them a lieutenant-general. It would be about as just to accuse Lee of undue partiality to Georgia in making Longstreet his senior lieutenant, as it is to accuse him of partiality to Virginia in selecting A. P. Hill rather than D. H. Hill or McLaws for the command of his Third Corps.

Second. In regard to the Battle of Gettysburg: The first day's fight was brought on unexpectedly to Lee. In the absence of Stuart, he was not aware of the proximity of the Federal Army. The first day's operations were very successful. Two of the seven infantry corps of the Federal army were virtually demolished, having been defeated and driven in disorder completely from the field, leaving many killed and wounded and several thousand prisoners to the victors.

Third. It was at the close of this day's work that General Lee, in view of its results, and of the indications it gave of the position of the Federal Army, decided to follow up the fight. General Longstreet advised a movement across Meade's front to threaten his left and rear. Such a movement would have been difficult in the absence of Stuart; it could not have been executed in the position then occupied by the army with sufficient prompt ness to surprise Meade; and if successful it simply would have forced the Federal Army back to some position nearer Baltimore and Washington where the issue of battle was still to be tried. General Longstreet begs the question when he assumes that Meade would then have been obliged to attack at a disadvantage.

General Lee decided that this plan did not promise as good results as to follow up the partial victory already gained. More than one-fourth of the Federal Army was beaten. (Of the First and Eleventh corps that had numbered 20,931 on June 30th, not 5700 were in line on July 2nd.) That army was not concentrated, and hours must elapse before its full strength could be marshalled for battle. The absent portions would reach the field jaded by forced marches, to meet the depressing news of the defeat of their comrades. Doubt and uncertainty would prevail, increased perhaps by the fact that the present Federal commander was so new in his place.

Lee's troops were much more nearly up, only Pickett's division and Law's brigade being out of reach. Not to press the Union Army was to lose the greater part of the advantage of the first day's victory. The Federals would soon recover from their depression if not pressed, and his own troops would be disappointed. Lee believed if he could attack early on the second day he would have but part of the Federal Army to deal with, and that if he could repeat his success of the first day the gain would be great. He therefore determined upon attack. On the night of the 1st (not on the forenoon of the 2nd, as General Longstreet has it) he decided, after a conference with Ewell and his division commanders, to make the attack early next day from his right with Longstreet's two divisions that were within reach, this attack to be supported by Hill and Ewell. (See Ewell's and Early's reports: Early's paper in *Southern Historical Society Papers*, Vol. IV.; and Long's *Memoirs of Lee*.)

Fourth. General Longstreet would have us infer that he was not ordered by General Lee to attack early on the second day; but that his memory is at fault on this point has been abundantly shown by Generals Fitz Lee, Pendleton, Early, Wilcox, and many others. No testimony on this point is more direct and conclusive than that of General A. L. Long, then military secretary to General Lee. He says in his recently published *Memoirs of R. E. Lee*), that on the evening of the 1st, when General Lee had decided not to renew the attack on Cemetery Hill that day, he said (in Long's presence) to Longstreet and Hill:

> Gentlemen, we will attack the enemy in the morning as early as practicable.

Long continues:

> In the conversation that succeeded he (Lee) directed them to make the necessary preparations and be ready for prompt action the next day.

Long shows plainly that General Lee's design was to attack the troops in front before the whole Federal army could get up, and he describes graphically the impatience Lee showed next morning, as early as 9 a. m., at Longstreet's delay. General Longstreet is wrong, too, in giving the impression that his divisions were fifteen or twenty miles away on the night of the 1st, for in his official report he says that:

> McLaws's division . . . reached Marsh Creek, four miles from Gettysburg, a little after dark, and Hood's division (except Law's brigade) got within nearly the same distance of the town about 12 o'clock at night.

Hood says he was with his staff "in front of the heights of Gettysburg shortly after daybreak" on the 2nd, and his troops were close behind. Kershaw (of McLaws's division) says in his official report that on the 1st of July they:

> Marched to a point on the Gettysburg road some two miles from that place, going into camp at 12 p. m.

General Longstreet, to explain his delay, besides the above reasons scrapes together a number of others,—such as the presence of some

Federal scouts and pickets west of the Emmitsburg road, the movement of Sickles's rear-guard along that road, the presence of one of General Lee's engineers (who had been sent to give information, not to command his corps). No time need be wasted on these. The fact is that General Longstreet, though knowing fully the condition of things on the night of the 1st, knowing that Lee had decided to attack that part of the Federal Army in his front, knowing that every hour strengthened Meade and diminished the chances of Confederate success, and knowing that his corps was to open the battle and deliver the main assault, consumed the time from daylight to nearly 4 p. m., on July 2nd, in moving his troops about four miles, over no serious obstacle, and in getting them into battle.

Meantime on the Federal side Hancock's corps, which had camped three miles from Gettysburg, reached the field by 6 or 7 a. m.; Sickles's two brigades that had been left at Emmitsburg came up by 9 a. m.; the rear of the Fifth Corps by midday, and the Sixth Corps, after a march of thirty-two miles in thirty hours, by 2 p. m. Had Longstreet attacked not later than 9 or 10 a. m., as Lee certainly expected, Sickles's and Hancock's corps would have been defeated before the Sixth Corps and part of the Fifth arrived. Little Round Top (which, as it was, the Fifth Corps barely managed to seize in time) would have fallen into Confederate possession; and even if nothing more had been done this would have given the field to the Confederates, since the Federal line all the way to Cemetery Hill was untenable with Round Top in hostile hands.

Fifth. That Longstreet's attack when made was poorly seconded by the other corps may be true, and thus another chance of winning a complete victory on July 2nd was lost, but this does not change the fact that the first and great opportunity of that day for the Confederates was lost by Longstreet's delay.

Sixth. Victory on the third day was for the Confederates a far more difficult problem than on the second, but it was still within their reach. But one need not be surprised at the failure of Pickett's attack after reading of the hesitation, the want of confidence and hearty cooperation, with which General Longstreet directed it. Lee never intended that Pickett, Pettigrew, and Trimble should fight unsupported by the remainder of the army. He expected "that with proper concert of action . . . we should ultimately succeed." (Lee's report.) Longstreet was directed to use his whole corps, and when he felt embarrassed by the

Federal forces on or near the Round Tops he was given a division and a half from A. P. Hill's corps, with power to call for more.

General Long says:

> The original intention of General Lee was that Pickett's attack should be supported by the divisions of McLaws and Hood, and General Longstreet was so ordered. (*Memoirs of Lee.* See also statements of Colonels Venable and Taylor, *Four Years with General Lee.*)

Lee's efforts for a concerted attack were ineffectual. Pickett was overwhelmed not by troops in front but by those on his flanks, especially by those on his right flank, where Wilcox was sent forward too late to be of use, and where he was too weak to have effected much at best. Yet Longstreet did not use any part of Hood's and McLaws's divisions to support Pickett, or to make a diversion in his favour, or to occupy the troops on his flank which finally defeated him. These divisions were practically idle, except that one of Hood's brigades was occupied in driving off the Federal cavalry which made a dash on that flank. Longstreet, in a word, sent forward one-third of his corps to the attack, but the remainder of his troops did not cooperate. And yet he reproaches Lee for the result!

McDonogh, Md., February 16th, 1887.

GROUND OVER WHICH PICKETT, PETTIGREW, AND TRIMBLE CHARGED. FROM A PHOTOGRAPH TAKEN SINCE THE WAR.

On the left of the picture (which shows the view from the Union lines) is seen the clump of trees which was the point of direction for Pickett's men; also the monument of Webb's brigade of Gibbon's division (Second Corps), near which General Alexander S. Webb was wounded. General Armistead, of Pickett's division, was killed in the middle foreground of the picture; Codori's house is seen on the right [see also map, p. 344].—EDITORS.

MAP of the BATTLE
of
GETTYSBURG
showing Positions held
JULY 1ST 2D & 3D 1863.

Union Lines.
Confederate "
Scale of 1 Mile.

A Soldier of the Civil War

By a member of the Virginia Historical Society

When Virginia was swept into the movement of secession and proudly took her position at the head of the column of seceding States it was natural that Captain Pickett, as a native of Virginia, should follow her leading, and should feel too that the path of honour and duty lay that way. So far as he was concerned there was no pretence of justification for the step upon constitutional grounds, although he was perfectly familiar, by virtue of his West Point training, with the principles of constitutional interpretation laid down to Rawle. He simply said:

> Proud as I am of the great name of American citizen, I cannot raise my arm against my own kith and kin.

But if fight they must, it was his earnestly expressed hope that they would fight under the old flag. He wanted the stars and stripes to float over the armies of the South.

In February, 1862, General Pickett was assigned by the Confederate government to the command of a Virginian brigade of infantry. With characteristic promptitude he pushed at once to the front, and, upon ground made historic by the surrender of Cornwallis, maintained unbroken a line of defence against the advancing forces of McClellan. At the Battle of Williamsburg his command not only checked the advance of that magnificent army, but actually drove it back. At Gaines' Mill he led the assault which broke the enemy's line. The situation, near sunset, was extremely critical.

"Something must be done," said Lee to Longstreet, "or the day is lost." The Federal line extended from Chickahominy to Cold Harbor. The position was naturally strong, and powerful batteries were planted at every dominant point. To save the day, the brigades of Pickett and

179

Anderson were ordered to an assault upon the formidable line of defences in front.

The battle was raging furiously; the enemy were holding their entrenchments with the tenacity of desperation, and one hundred and twenty guns were hurling a destructive fire upon the column of advance. But nothing could resist the determined and impetuous fury of the assault. Pickett, shot from his horse, paused but a moment, and pressing forward on foot still led his dauntless brigade, the riderless horse following close, as if the animal's master still held the rein.

The charge was resistless, and the field was won. The strong blue line recoils; the reserves give way; the faithful gunners are swept from their guns; the contested ground is seized and held by the Confederate column of assault; McClellan's disciplined legions are driven tumultuously into the Chickahominy swamps, and Lee with his whole army is in hot pursuit. The Federal commander, whose patient genius for war was even then preparing the way for ultimate success, was only saved from utter rout by the roads and bridges which he had constructed for a victorious Federal advance. Pickett's and Anderson's brigades had not only saved the day but had shed imperishable glory upon the Confederate arms. The attack in front was made by these brigades alone.

General Pickett's wound was severe enough to keep him from the field for several months, and when he rejoined his brigade, in September, he was still unable to bear the pressure of a sleeve. In the fight at Frazier's Farm, three days after the Battle of Gaines' Mill, the general's brother. Major Charles Pickett, was shot down while carrying the colours at the head of the advancing brigade. He "wanted to be in at the finish," he said, and he almost realised his wish. The gallant young soldier was disabled for life.

★★★★★★

General Pickett was assigned to the command of a division in September, 1862, and on the 10th of the following month was promoted to the rank of major-general. In the reorganisation of the army which followed the return from the Maryland campaign, the brigades of Pickett, Kemper, and Jenkins were consolidated into a division, to which, later, Armistead's brigade was attached, and Major-General Pickett was assigned to the permanent command, the division as now constituted forming part of Longstreet's corps. Its first appearance upon the field was at the Battle of Fredericksburg, December 13, 1862, when it was held in reserve with instructions from Longstreet simply to "hold the ground in defence" conjointly with the division of Hood, unless they could see an opportunity to attack the enemy while engaged with A. P. Hill on the right.

At the first moment of the break on Jackson's lines (says Longstreet) Pickett, eager to strike the Federal column as it advanced in the open field, rode to Hood and urged that the opportunity anticipated was at hand, but Hood "failed to see it in time for effective work." His failure was a subject of critical remark and even reported in the official accounts. Hood stood in high favour with the authorities at Richmond, and the biographer of President Davis says that he was "the noblest contribution of the chivalry of Kentucky to the armies of the South."

The division of Pickett was held in reserve, therefore, but straining at the leash and impatient for the signal to advance. The gallant division waited long—many months, indeed, but it did not wait in vain. The opportunity came at last.

The renowned legions of Longstreet and Ewell (the latter in command of Jackson's old corps) abandoned their position near Fredericksburg on the third day of June, leaving A. P. Hill on guard along the line of the Rappahannock, watching ford and ferry and vigilantly confronting the forces of the Federal commander. General Hooker, who has signally failed to grasp the strategic significance of the situation in front, and, wholly oblivious of the campaign in progress, is meditating with the solicitude of a true soldier upon the prospective operations of General Lee. Days elapse, and on the 22nd of June, General Hooker is still in quest of information concerning the movements or his great antagonist, and the electric wires are flashing his notes of interrogation to every point, "Have any of the enemy's infantry," he asks General Tyler, in command at Maryland Heights, "marched north from the Potomac?"

"Do they continue to cross?" he asks again on the following day. He is clearly not satisfied with the assurance given by his chief of staff that Lee's movement upon the Potomac is a mere cover for a cavalry raid; nor with the scandalous suggestion of Pleasanton a stout fighter—that they are still in the Shenandoah Valley, and will remain there as long as they are permitted to "steal supplies" from the adjoining states. Still less can he be induced to believe that the movement is simply a wild dash of Confederate foragers, and that the "whole population of the country—generals and all"—are crazed with a panic and "stricken with a heavy stampede."

When Tyler received Hooker's telegram on the 22nd, the Confederate camp-fires were already ablaze upon the banks of the Potomac. Ewell boldly leading the old Stonewall corps, has crossed the river and is marching northward with Imboden's cavalry on his left wing, the cavalry of Stuart on his right, and the first division of A. P. Hill's corps moving up rapidly in his rear. Hooker may have been slow in his perceptions, but he was prompt to act; when the emergency was pressing none could be more alert or bold. He was a soldier upon instinct. His cavalry were "out," he said, "feeling up to the enemy and hard at work." He ordered Heintzelman to seize the South Mountain Pass and hold it at all hazards; the first corps was ordered to seize and occupy Crampton's Pass; and Stahel's command was directed to move at once toward Gettysburg and Frederick, and "drive from the country every rebel in it."

On the 24th day of June the chief engineer of the Army of the Potomac (Warren) submitted to the Federal commander some cogent strategic reasons for moving the army immediately to the neighbourhood of Harper's Ferry. "It is the straightest line to reach Lee's army," he said, "and will enable us to paralyze his movements by striking his flank and rear." In the orders which Hooker gave he seems to have adopted these views at once. The mountain passes were directed to be seized and held. The possibility of such a movement had been anticipated by Lee. On the 19th of June he writes to Ewell:

> Longstreet is manoeuvring to detain Hooker east of the mountains until A. P. Hill can come up in support of the Confederate advance. Should the enemy force a passage through the mountains you would be separated from A, P. Hill, and it is this separation of forces that Longstreet is striving to prevent.

Not knowing what force is at Harper's Ferry, and having no definite information as to the movements of General Hooker, the Confederate commander does not feel that he is in position to advise; but should Hooker be drawn across the river by Ewell's advance, he assures Ewell that Longstreet will follow at once. It is evident that the strategic conceptions of Hooker and his chief of engineers were anticipated in the reflections of General Lee.

The report of Warren to Hooker advising the movement upon Harper's Ferry was dated at Stafford Court-House, June 24. Hooker lost no time in moving upon the lines indicated in the report of his engineer. On the 25th and 26th of June he crossed the Potomac at

Edward's Ferry. He marched at once to Frederick, and arranging to reinforce Slocum with the troops at Harper's Ferry, he expected to push rapidly through the western passes and fall upon the flank and rear of Lee—precisely as Lee had hypothetically prognosticated, and as Warren had actually proposed. "Troops from Harper's Ferry! No," was the peremptory response of Halleck; "the troops must not be taken from Harper's Ferry; the Maryland Heights must be held as the key to Maryland."

"But why hold the key," said the injudicious Hooker, "when the door has been smashed in?" The only response to this felicitous counter-stroke was the official announcement from Washington that General Hooker had been relieved from his command.

On the day that Hooker was relieved, the 27th of June, the vanguard of Lee under Ewell moved from Chambersburg to Carlisle. Sixty thousand Confederate veterans were now upon Pennsylvanian soil, seeking a decisive conflict upon a Northern field with the magnificent army which had been trained by the disciplinary genius of McClellan, and after many reverses was now rallying with incredible swiftness under the leadership of the intrepid and soldierly Meade.

It is worthy of special remark that one of the first acts of the new commander-in-chief was an incidental vindication of his gallant predecessor. He ordered the immediate withdrawal of the ten thousand troops from Harper's Ferry. They were withdrawn and placed in active service at once. Hooker was vindicated; the army was seasonably reinforced; and Halleck was apparently justified in his estimate of the military capacity of Meade—the latest Federal protagonist projected into the arena of war.

The commands of Longstreet and Ewell, as we have seen, abandoned the line of the Rappahannock on the 3rd day of June.

On the 18th of June, 1863 (a notable anniversary in the annals of war), Lee with sixty thousand disciplined veterans and two hundred effective guns crossed the Potomac and swept northward, pouring a tide of invasion directly into the heart of the loyal states. The field of conflict was transferred at once to Northern soil, as yet untouched by the hand of war. In less than ten days the Southern army was threatening an advance upon the capital of the state—possibly upon the capital of the United States; but wherever it went and whatever it did, or failed to do, this is certainly true, that the hand of the spoiler was stayed by a strong and peremptory order from Lee. No retaliation, he said, no robbery, no spoliation, outrage or waste.

"We make war only upon armed men." If the needy invaders paid for supplies in Confederate scrip, it was with the conscientious assumption that ultimately the discredited paper would be made good by Confederate success.

Not the least, then, of the glories of the Gettysburg campaign was the famous General Order No. 73. It registers the high-water mark of modern civilized war.

On the 28th day of June, General Lee issued an order directing an immediate concentration of his forces at Cashtown, which lies east of the mountains and near the northern extremity of the valley where the battle of Gettysburg was fought. At the entrance of this narrow valley lies Gettysburg itself—a natural strategic centre to which all roads seem to lead; and toward this compelling centre gathered the converging forces as by the operation of a natural law. Among the roads radiating from the mountain village is a broad thoroughfare leading toward the northwest. It is the Chambersburg road, and it was at or near the town of Chambersburg that Pickett's division was left to guard the trains and secure the rear. There it remained until the 2nd day of July.

It is told that when this gallant division was moving northward through the prosperous farming regions of Southern Pennsylvania, they were greeted at one of the pretty villages in an old German settlement through which they passed by an enthusiastic little maid, who stood with the national flag in her hand, defiantly waving it at the advancing column and flaunting it directly under the eyes of the Confederate commander who was riding ahead. Instantly the Southern leader wheeled from the line, doffed his cap with easy grace, and bowing to the little patriot, respectfully saluted the flag she bore. Turning, he lifted his hand, and as the splendid column passed every veteran doffed his cap in chivalric salute to the national banner and the heroic little maid. When afterward asked how he could bring himself to salute the enemy's flag, the Confederate leader replied:

No, not the enemy's flag; I saluted the glorious banner of my youth, and the heroic womanhood in the heart of a young girl.

For two mortal days the eager and impatient veterans of Pickett lay within a few hours' march of the battle that was imminent or raging upon the mountain ridges to the east; and it was not until the morning of the 2nd of July that the division which was to become exceptionally conspicuous upon that field received orders from Gettysburg to join its corps. A march of twenty-four miles under a burning July sun brought Pickett's division within three miles of Gettysburg, where they halted at 2 o'clock in the afternoon, their commander promptly reporting their arrival to General Lee, and asking but two hours' rest to put them in thorough readiness for service in the field.

He then rode at once to meet Longstreet, the commander of the corps—noting the little town of Gettysburg on the left as he passed into the valley, and the two parallel ridges upon which the contending armies were encamped—the Federal forces upon "Cemetery" Ridge looking west, the Confederates upon "Seminary" Ridge looking east, the town of Gettysburg lying between. He found Longstreet in the midst of battle, and greatly relieved by the arrival of his Virginian brigades. "I always feel certain and sure," said the gallant old warrior, "of Pickett and Pickett's men."

Over the ridge they rode thoughtfully together, watching the fight in front of Little Round Top, and studying the field for the fight to-morrow. Lee had achieved, as he said in his report, "partial successes;" he had gained some ground; the enemy had suffered heavy losses; his own army was still formidable and well in hand; and, with that fatal contempt for a luckless and awkward adversary which infected even the soul of Lee, the Confederate commander was ready for another and final assault upon the following day.

Everywhere throughout the army it was understood that Pickett and his splendid division would make the assault; and as early as 3 o'clock on the morning of the 3rd it was under arms behind the crest and forming a line of battle facing Cemetery Ridge, a little to the left of Meade's centre; Kemper on the right, Garnett on the left, Armistead directly in the rear—a division of less than five thousand men. When the attacking column was complete the division of Pettigrew was on the left of Pickett's division; to the left and rear of Pettigrew were the two brigades of Trimble. Anderson and Wilcox were ordered to support the column of assault. The line formed, the men were ordered to lie down in the deep grass and keep still. And there they lay until deep in the shadows of the westering sun.

During the struggle that was now in progress for the possession of Culp's Hill, the rugged eminence to the east which formed the right of Meade's crescentic line, Pickett stood with Longstreet and Lee on the summit of Seminary Ridge, as on the previous day he had stood with Longstreet alone noting the assault upon Little Round Top, the left of Meade's compact, projecting, curvilinear front. Today his own

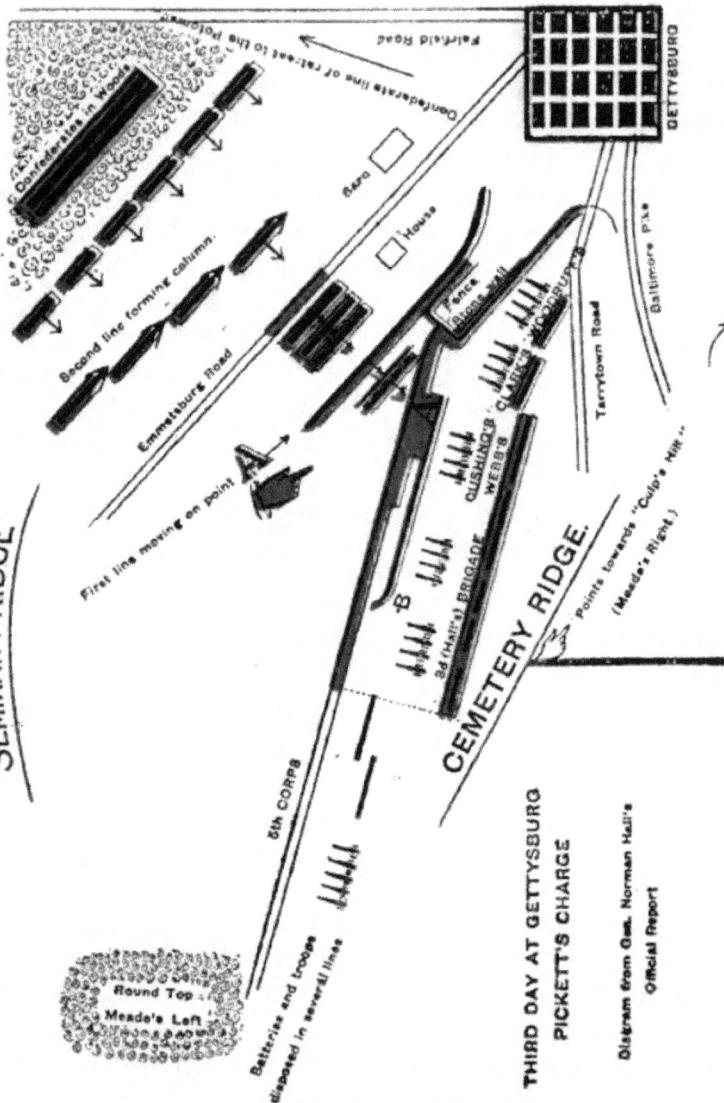

SEMINARY RIDGE

Confederates in Woods

Second line forming column.

First line moving on point

Emmetsburg Road

Fairfield Road

Confederate line of retreat to the Potomac

GETTYSBURG

Barn

House

Fence Stone wall

WOODRUFF'S

CLARKS

Baltimore Pike

Tarrytown Road

CUSHING'S

WEBB'S

3d (HALL'S) BRIGADE

B

Points towards "Culp's Hill."
(Meade's Right.)

CEMETERY RIDGE.

5th CORPS

Batteries and troops
disposed in several lines

Round Top
Meade's Left

THIRD DAY AT GETTYSBURG
PICKETT'S CHARGE

Diagram from Gen. Norman Hall's
Official Report

division will deliver the assault upon Meade's centre; and the series of independent, unsupported, and unsuccessful assaults upon the Federal entrenchments will be complete. The scene before the opening of the battle was one of idyllic peace. The morning sun was pouring a flood of light into every nook of the narrow valley; the air was beginning to shimmer with excess of heat, and the almost vertical rays of sunlight were suffused with a reddish flame that seemed not only to smite but sear. The luxuriance of midsummer was crowning every summit and brightening every slope, and the leafage of the woodlands was taking a deeper and a richer hue.

Cattle were browsing peacefully upon the shaded slopes of the eastern hills, or ruminating drowsily in the shadows of the woodland trees; orchards were bending and aglow with their burdens of summer fruit; the golden wheat fields were aflame with the radiance of the morning sun; the murmurous life of midsummer was in the quivering air; and, innocently oblivious of impending battle, flocks of migratory pigeons were circling over all. But the three Confederate leaders, intent upon other thoughts, were making a personal reconnaissance of the situation in front—the long line of lowland, the threatening slope and summit stretching toward the north, and the embattled hill-tops confronting their lines upon the east—a fine historic group for a great artist as they sat upon their horses, like cavaliers in bronze, their erect, soldierly figures rising boldly above the summit of the ridge and sharply outlined against the morning sky.

They gazed upon the scene with an intentness that bespoke the interest that they felt; and, if sagacity and experience in war could reveal what they sought, they might easily have wrested the secrets of destiny from what they saw in the long reaches of the valley, upon the rugged eastern slopes, upon the rocky salients frowning like bastions upon the projected line of advance, and upon the central convexity of the long crescentic ridge entrenched to the sky-line with batteries that seemed to make it almost impregnable to assault. Between the Confederate line and the proposed point of attack were ridges and roads and streams, a strong stone wall, post-and-rail fences, streaks or swale, and low, steep hills. In the shadows of the distant ridge were two tiers of guns, supported by soldiers or unflinching resolution and served by gunners of experience and skill.

The reserves of infantry, the flower of the Federal host, were in double columns near the crest, screened and protected by the solid stone wall that skirts the lower slope. The line of advance was also obstructed by a strong post-and-rail fence in the plain below. This was the position to be taken by assault, and the Confederate leaders did not underrate the seriousness and magnitude of the attempt. Longstreet had tested the practicability of the assault the day before. A renewal of the attempt would require close co-operation of the entire Confederate line and a minimum force of thirty thousand men. "The fifteen thousand men," he said, "who could make a successful assault over that field had never been arrayed for battle."

But Lee was obstinate, and Pickett was confident of success. With leaders and men alike, "strong battle was in the air."

The Confederate column of assault lies in long, silent ranks in the tall grass, and they rise and salute silently as the commanders pass in thoughtful review, honoured and touched by the homage they receive and proud of the source from which it comes. The assaulting column was well chosen for the work. The soldiers that composed it were the flower of the Virginian infantry and the pride of the warlike Confederacy whose flag they bore. Not surly zealots moulded into soldiers by the iron discipline of Cromwellian war; far less, swaggering and dissolute cavaliers clinging desperately to the fortunes of a falling house. They were neither profligates nor fanatics; and yet they had the soldierly virtues of both the Roundhead and the Cavalier. Offspring of a generous English breed, cradled in Christian homes and reared within sound of the church-going bell; with spirits finely touched by the subtle influences of a Virginian environment, and inspired by ideals drawn from the highest traditions of their race, it was a thoroughly disciplined host of patient, high-bred, resolute.

God-fearing men, fighting, as they devoutly believed, for the honour, for the rights, for the existence of that ancient state to which they were as loyal as a cavalier to his king. The earliest escutcheon of the Old Dominion was quartered with the arms of the Stuart dynasty, but the earliest political charter of the Commonwealth of Virginia was charged with the principles of civil and religious liberty which drove the despotic Stuart from his throne. In laying the political foundations of Virginia, Sir Edwin Sandys had placed a Genevan stamp upon Church and State; and, building upon the lines of his ideal commonwealth, had trained its people in a rigid republican school. (*The Genesis of the United States*: Dr. Alexander Brown).

The austere virtues of the founders were transmitted to their children, and the seasoned warriors who are standing upon the perilous edge of battle at Gettysburg today, (1900), are typical representatives of much that was best in the generations of the past. They are not the *janizaries* of a "barbarous patriciate," as an eloquent Spanish statesman would have had the world believe, but the military elite of a free Anglican commonwealth, which even in its cradle defied the malice and machinations of a Spanish king. Cromwell himself would have been proud to lead the men who charge at Gettysburg this day; and when it is told that the favourite hymn of their daring commander—of the man who had led them through a tempest of fire at Gaines' Mill— was the familiar Christian lyric, *Guide me, O Thou Great Jehovah*, that old- world hymn sung over cradles by generations of Virginian mothers—it helps us to form some conception of the devout and trustful nature of this indomitable soldier of the South. The simple lines of that old Protestant hymn are touched with the true prophetic fire, and its awful imagery, "Death of Death and Hell's destruction," might well appeal to the imagination of the Virginian soldier who led the charge on that tremendous day.

The men are, indeed, well chosen for the work, and the leader is worthy of the men; and his generals are worthy of their chief—Garnett, who served with Stonewall Jackson; Armistead, who charged in generous rivalry with Pickett at Chapultepec; and Kemper, who in the Seven Days' battles led the old Longstreet brigade. Pickett himself was finely and generously characterized by McClellan, the Federal commander, as "the incomparable *paladin* of the far-famed infantry of the South."

"Give George Pickett an order," said a veteran Confederate officer, "and he will storm the gates of hell."

The ridge upon which Meade's lines were extended may be likened in its general curvilinear course to the outline of that familiar pastoral implement, an English shepherd's crook, the Federal left resting upon a knobbed handle at the Round Top and the right upon the terminal querl at Culp's Hill, that section of the shaft between Cemetery Hill, near Gettysburg on the north, and the wooded heights of Round Top on the south representing Meade's main or west front— looking directly westward upon Seminary Ridge and in close touch at the rear with the Federal east-front at Culp's Hill, on the right Near the left centre of the main or west-front is the point selected by Lee for the assault.

Glancing eastward from the Confederate position, we note that the distance to be covered by the charging column is scarcely less than three-quarters of a mile; the distance from the Confederate batteries to the Federal position on Cemetery Hill does not exceed fourteen hundred yards; the entire area of the field upon which the drama unfolds does not exceed a mile square—actually limiting the space upon which the column is to be developed and extended for the charge. Along the crest of the ledge-like elevations at the foot of Seminary Ridge, corresponding to similar elevations at the base of Cemetery Ridge, is a line of one hundred and forty-five Confederate guns. Alexander's battery of seventy-five guns is on an elevation near the Emmitsburg Road; Walker's sixty-three guns are posted to the left of Alexander on Seminary Ridge. The attacking column was ordered to advance under cover of the continued fire of these guns. The batteries were in position by 10 o'clock in the morning. Lee had ordered batteries to be pushed forward with the infantry to protect their flanks and support their attacks, and Alexander held nine howitzers in reserve, intending to push them ahead of Pickett's line of advance nearly up to musket-range.

These guns were removed just before the advance without his sanction or knowledge; other guns were provided, but ammunition was scant, and the assaulting column pushed forward on the afternoon of the 3rd was practically unprotected by guns. The Confederate artillery for the preliminary assault on the Federal centre was in position on the crest of a ridge nearly parallel to the enemy's line which was formed on a corresponding elevation on Cemetery Ridge, a distance of nearly one mile. For a distance of two miles, the line of Confederate batteries "covered," or commanded the enemy's western front—stretching from a point opposite the town of Gettysburg to the Peach Orchard which closed the view to the left, "Never," said the Federal Chief of Artillery, " had such a sight been witnessed on this continent, and rarely, if ever, abroad."

At 1 o'clock the signal-guns broke silence and the Confederate batteries, which were massed at the edge of the woods, opened a direct, continuous, undeviating fire upon the entrenched line between the cemetery and the right of the Fifth Corps, which was at a distance of several hundred yards from the Federal left at Round Top. A hundred guns upon Cemetery Ridge flashed back an instant response. Every crest is clouded with smoke and aflame with flashes of volcanic light; the hills and valleys are reverberant with the deep and continuous roar of two hundred guns. A storm of deadly missiles fills the clouded air, and the low valley is suffocating with the hot breath of war; the shells from the cemetery passing over the line of artillery, and exploding as they pass the reclining ranks of the Confederate infantry, search the sheltering coverts with destructive effect.

The Federal infantry on Cemetery Ridge cling to the shelter of the solid stone wall near the summit; but the space in the rear of the crest is swept with deadly effect by the fire of the Confederate guns. The Federal camp is a scene of indescribable confusion. The general headquarters were a hopeless wreck, the army trains were in wild retreat, and a horde of frantic camp followers was rolling tumultuously to the rear.

"Never," says the Federal General Walker, "had so dreadful a storm burst upon mortal men."

The Federal Army closely massed upon a contracted ridge (a result of the recent operations of Lee) were in a favourable position to test the effects of the convergent Confederate fire, which only ceased when the ammunition failed, after two hours of terrific war. A half hour of silence and deadly suspense and the attacking column begins to form, just below the brow of Seminary Ridge, in long double lines debouching from valleys, ravines, and woody coverts, and failing rapidly into a formidable column of attack, thirteen thousand strong, two separate lines of double ranks, formed one hundred yards apart; in the centre, Pickett's division the veteran brigades of Garnett, Armistead, and Kemper) selected to deliver the assault in front, the division of Pettigrew and Trimble supporting the advance upon the left; the command of Wilcox, in columns of battalions, following on the right.

As Pickett rode up to Longstreet for orders, a courier advanced hurriedly with a note. It is from Alexander, the Chief of Artillery. The ammunition is failing; the situation is pressing; and there is no slackening of the enemy's fire.

"If you are coming," said Alexander to Pickett, "come at once."

Pickett turned to Longstreet. "General, shall I advance?"

There was no response, and, awaiting none, Pickett said, "I will lead my division forward."

And the extraordinary march began. For once, at least, without an order, "he would storm the gates of hell."

The veteran Longstreet, deeply moved, said nothing. He could only bow assent to the imperative orders of Lee. Writing thirty-four years afterward, he still sees in memory the gallant soldier as he rides into battle on that memorable day—glorious as young Harry with his cuisses on—of medium height, of graceful figure, of magnetic presence, and incomparable in all the accomplishments of war. Doubtless, too, the veteran recalls another day, in another land, and a desperate assault under another flag, when a young lieutenant seized the colours which a wounded comrade had dropped, and under a deadly fire, triumphantly planted them on the captured heights. The young lieutenant was Pickett, and the wounded comrade Longstreet.

Today, too, when Longstreet falters, Pickett seizes the drooping colours and bears them in triumph to the flaming crest of Cemetery Ridge. There is a passing flutter along the line, and the magnificent column begins to move—launched straight at the Federal centre. Near the middle of Hancock's line is a clump of trees. This had been indicated by Lee as the objective point of attack, and toward this point the column is now moving as if each soldier were a centre of resistless force. The strong individuality of the Southern soldier is manifest at every step. The tall, lithe, erect figure; the bold, resolute air; the strong, spare, sinewy physique; the leopard-like elasticity of frame; and the calm, penetrating intelligence of the eye all bespeak the evolution of another type. It is the Anglo-Virginian type evolved by conditions antedating the war. Sir Charles Dilke "looked instinctively for baldrick and rapier" when he saw these Confederate veterans in the piping times of peace.

As soon as Pickett, emerging from the woods on the reverse slope, passes the crest of the hill, the Federal batteries open fire; and a strong continuous flight of shell, passing over the line of Confederate batteries, falls upon the advancing column with deadly effect. As he descends the eastern slope of Seminary Ridge, the column encounters a combined fire from Round Top on the Federal left and from the batteries directly in front. As the column passes the marshy tract in the field below, a line of infantry moves down upon the left flank. Beyond this point they encounter a destructive fire from the Federal sharp-shooters; and this is followed, as the field opens, by a terrific fire of musketry from the front, and a deadly enfilade from the rifled guns on Round Top.

Two armies are watching with breathless interest every step of the awful march. From the moment the glorious column takes shape upon the wooded crest of Seminary Ridge, until it disappears in the lurid clouds of battle in the east, not a detail of the magnificent movement is lost. On, on they come: a double line of skirmishers; the line of battle for the charge; another line of battle in reserve. Shells from the Federal batteries on Cemetery Ridge drop destructively on the advancing column; and, as it descends the slope with stately, measured

PICKETT'S CHARGE, I.—LOOKING DOWN THE UNION LINES FROM THE "CLUMP OF TREES."
General Hancock and staff are seen in the left center of the picture.

tread, it is torn by round shot plunging through its ranks; the Emmitsburg road is reached, the Federal skirmishers fall back, the fire of the Confederate batteries ceases; and, as the unwavering column advances, a concentrated fire is poured from ridge and Round Top directly upon flank and front.

Halfway over the field they halt in a ravine to rest, and reform for the final charge. As it resumes the advance, a clear ringing order of Pickett, "Left oblique," changes the direction of the column from the front to the left, and at once from the batteries on Cemetery Ridge, a fire from forty cannon is poured upon the exposed right flank. It is like the scythe of death. "Front forward!" again comes a clear, trumpet-like command, and in an instant the indomitable column is sweeping upon the centre as before, but now, in the midst of a concentrated fire from the Federal guns on Cemetery Ridge, from the infantry behind the Federal works, and from the enfilading batteries on Round Top, a wild, destructive storm of round shot, shells, shrapnel, canister, and grape.

The slaughter is appalling. Kemper falls desperately wounded. Garnett Keeps his head, and raising his mighty voice, in vibrant tones steadies the shattered column, and cheers the unfaltering advance. From behind the stone wall a withering fire of musketry is pouring into the devoted column, which promptly responds, with a deadly precision of aim. "Cease firing," cries Garnett, "save your strength."

At once the disciplined veterans reload their guns and shoulder arms, yet not for one instant slackening the pace of that triumphant advance. The post-and-rail fence gives but a moment's pause. The entire column glides over it as lightly as a sportsman, in quest of game. On, on they press, the movement quickened by the concentrated fire of a hundred guns.

"Pickett moved among his men," says an eyewitness, "as if he courted death by his reckless daring."

The rain of deadly missiles never ceases, and the Federal parapet on the heights is fringed with fire from end to end. In the midst of the wild tempest beating from the hilltop, these incomparable soldiers preserve their company formation, and respond to commands as if upon parade or review, halting, aligning, reforming their thinned and bleeding ranks; and, at last, in perfect line, pressing steadily forward, Armistead's brigade closing up m staunch support, they suddenly dash with a wild cry, at a double-quick, and under a deadly cross-fire, upon guns-shotted to the muzzle, and charged with destruction for the ad-

PICKETT'S CHARGE, II.—THE MAIN COLLISION TO THE RIGHT OF THE "CLUMP OF TREES."

In this hand-to-hand conflict General Armistead, of Pickett's Division, was killed, and General Webb, of Gibbon's Division, was wounded.

PICKETT'S CHARGE, III.

vancing ranks.

"Here," says General Gibbon, "the contest raged with almost unparalleled ferocity for nearly an hour."

At point blank range, the Federal commander with perfect deliberation, gives the command to fire, and the Confederate Line seems "literally to melt" under the crash of eighteen thousand guns. But the second line moves steadily up; every gap in the line of attack is closed as soon as made; the shattered division sweeps relentlessly over the fiery crest; the enemy, lifted from their feet by the impetuous rush, fall back from their smoking guns, and, for one inspiring quarter of an hour, the blue flag of Virginia is seen floating from the summit of Cemetery Ridge!

But it was a fleeting triumph. The resistless wave of battle which sweeps over the entrenched front of the ridge, clings for an instant, as if lapping the bloodstained crest, and rapidly recedes when its initial force is spent. The Federal infantry held their position with desperate tenacity, and the heroic gunners handled their batteries with consummate skill.

★★★★★★

Colonel Andrew Cowan, whose battery was with General Webb on the right, says in his report:

"The rebel line advanced in a most splendid manner. The infantry in front of five of my pieces and posted behind a slight defence of rails, some ten yards distant, turned and broke, but were rallied by General Webb . . . in a most gallant manner. It was then I fired my last charge of canister, many of the rebels being over the defences and within less than ten yards of my pieces." They were "literally swept." he says, from the Federal front.

★★★★★★

The Federal commanders divide the bloody honours of the battle with the leaders of the bold assault. Hancock and Gibbon were wounded while personally directing the defence; and Cushing, from the old Bay State, was killed while pushing his last gun to the front and driving the last canister into Armistead's advancing ranks. Armistead dies with his hand resting upon one of Cushing's guns, and the two heroes fall together, immortalised by their mutual antagonism and linked in an eternal embrace. (General Hancock says that he was "wounded with a tenpenny nail,"—an indication, he thought, that the Confederate ammunition was getting short).

For a time, consternation reigned in the Federal camp, and organisation was almost wholly lost. The line of General Webb was crumpled up on the right, and many men belonging to other commands, says the Federal commander, Hall, "were making to the rear as fast as possible, while the enemy were pouring over the rail fence." Finding two regiments or another command on the left, he tried to move them by the right flank to the break in the line, but coming under a hot fire, they crowded to the slight shelter of the rail fence, refusing to come out and reform. He was then forced to order his own brigade back from the line and move forward by the flank under a heavy fire. "The enemy," he says, "was rapidly gaining a foothold; organisation was mostly lost; in the confusion commands were useless." But, finally, by desperate efforts, the threatened retreat was stayed.

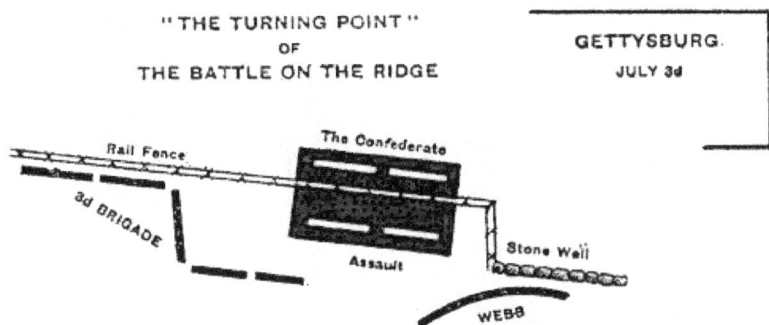

"THE TURNING POINT"
OF
THE BATTLE ON THE RIDGE

GETTYSBURG.
JULY 3d

(This diagram is, in its essential features, an exact reproduction of the diagram in Gen. Norman Hall's official report.)

The Federal veterans rallied gallantly on the second line, steadily reformed, poured a destructive fire into the captured works, and closed with their daring assailants in a deadly hand-to-hand fight. The invincible division of Pickett soon lapsed into a forlorn hope. Generals, colonels, and officers of all grades went down in the unequal fight, and a score of Confederate battle-flags were captured in a space of one hundred yards' square. A mere remnant of the division clung to the bloody ridge. Wilcox had failed to support the advance; Pettigrew's men had fled; and Anderson only moved when the assault had failed. Even when Wilcox moved forward (thirty minutes after Pickett's advance) there "was no longer anything to support." The gallant Trimble advancing under a destructive cross-fire in front and on both flanks, opened fire upon the enemy when in easy range, drove the artillerists from their guns, and only gave way when the whole force on his right was gone.

The troops that wavered in the advance, soon broke ranks and fell back in disorder, and at once an overwhelming force is thrown upon Pickett's flanks and front. The time for effective support was past; and Longstreet ordered Anderson's advancing division to halt. Stuart's resolute and well-sustained dash upon Meade's right was almost lost sight of in the overshadowing interest of Pickett's charge; and his repulse though decisive, is even now scarcely included among the disasters of the day. It was neither helpful as a diversion nor seriously embarrassing as a defeat. But the leadership was brilliant and the fighting superb.

It is said that on the third day at Gettysburg the Confederates lost sixty *per cent* of the assaulting forces. But it is hardly possible to give arithmetical expression to the statement or an irreparable loss. It furnishes some conception, however, of the desperate character of the charge to say that of fourteen field officers, but one remained. The men lay dead in heaps. A contemporary chronicler says:

> Looking around for his supports Pickett found himself alone.

His gallant comrades had helplessly fallen in an unequal conflict, and the appealing blasts of the paladin's bugle are still echoing among the passes of the hills. Who was it that had failed to respond when honour and duty were calling in this crisis of a people's fate? This we cannot say; nor is it needful that we should know that which Lee declared should remain unknown; but certain it is that Pickett's magnificent division—the pride of Virginia, and the glory of the South—was hopelessly shattered in one brief hour. In that immortal charge glory and disaster rode arm in arm. It was a bloody repulse for the division of Pickett; it was a serious reverse for the army of Lee; it was an irretrievable disaster for the cause of the South.

Slowly and sullenly the bleeding and tattered remnant of the command retires from the disastrous field; but the sentiment of American citizenship in its highest sense forbids us to say that, even for the vanquished, that day was lost. In the heart of the Confederate leader there was sorrow enough, but there was none of the bitterness, or the rancour, or the hopelessness of defeat. "Would that we had never crossed the Potomac," he said, "or that our splendid army had not been fought in detail."

Confronted at the opening of the civil conflict by a divided duty, he had met an imperative demand and had met it in a manly and resolute way. In a purely dramatic aspect, his career as a soldier was now rounded and complete. But he did not exalt himself. He gave the true measure of his greatness when he said: "I have done nothing; my men have done it all."

★★★★★★

An officer who was on the staff of General Rhodes says that when he saw Pickett falling back from the charge, he was walking beside General Kemper gently fanning the wounded brigadier as he was carefully borne from the field.

★★★★★★

If mere eulogy could add to the glory of Pickett and his men, what can exceed in pathetic eloquence the simple speech of Lincoln as he stood at the foot of Cemetery Ridge? Someone had reverently said: "Think of the men who held these heights."

"And think," said Lincoln, "of the men who stormed these heights."

Standing upon the same consecrated spot, and, speaking words that in solemn and impressive beauty recall that diviner discourse upon the Mount, Abraham Lincoln declared that the dead of Gettysburg had not died in vain and that, under God, there would be "a new birth of freedom for all." Even while he spoke, he must have felt, as his thoughts recurred to the past, how strange and mysterious had been the ways of Providence in the selection of instruments for the work to which he himself had dedicated his life. Scarcely a quarter of a century had elapsed, since a young Virginian with an hereditary bent toward the profession of arms, had been appointed through the influence of Mr. Lincoln, a friend of his family, to the military academy at West Point. Mr. Lincoln, writing familiarly to the boy, said:

"You see; I should like to have a perfect soldier credited to dear old Illinois."

And writing again, after his admission to the academy, Mr. Lincoln said:

The only victory that we can ever hope to call complete, will be the one which proclaims there is not a slave on God's green earth.

The young cadet thus carefully launched into a military career was George Edward Pickett, who was then preparing, under the eye of Lincoln himself, to enact a part upon the stage of American affairs, of which the great Emancipator little dreamed. With a depth of affection that to the common mind passes all understanding, the heart of the great statesman went out to his wayward *protégé* to the very end.

The Southern Confederacy was crumbling under the ceaseless and crushing assaults of Grant, and the stupendous drama of civil war was hastening rapidly to a close. With the surrender of the Confederate capital came the proclamation of peace.

After the surrender of Richmond, there stood one morning at the door of the old Pickett home, a tall, strong-visaged stranger, with careworn features, and a kindly light in his large, melancholy eyes. In the street, before the door, is a carriage with retinue and guard. It is apparently a visitor of note. A servant responds to the bell, but the visitor's inquiry is answered by a lady who comes to the door with an infant in her arms. "I am George Pickett's wife," she said.

"And I," said the stranger in a deep, sympathetic voice, "am Abraham Lincoln."

"The President?" she asked.

"No," was the prompt response, "Abraham Lincoln, George's old friend."

And then some kindly words to George's child, which touched the mother's heart. A few days later, George Pickett received the announcement of the President's tragical and untimely death. The indomitable Spirit of the Confederate veteran was crushed, and, remembering only the Lincoln he had loved, he cried out from his very heart, "My God! My God! The South has lost her best friend."

To say that Abraham Lincoln was not faultless is merely to say that he was not divine; to insist that he was not far-sighted and sagacious, is to suggest that he was divinely inspired. If he sometimes erred in his conceptions of the military situation, he erred with men who were presumed to be masters in the art of war. In vain we look among the children of men for infallibility either in statesmanship or the strategic art. Imperial Caesar sometimes slept. The greatest captains sometimes err. Nothing is more fickle than the fortune of war. Nevertheless, Abraham Lincoln was an incomparable leader of men; and, while McClellan and Grant could direct more or less successfully the operations of a hundred thousand men in the field.

It was Abraham Lincoln alone that could hold in hand the vast and turbulent electorate of eighteen Northern States, This was the host, in its more dangerous aspects a coalition of fanaticism and greed, which the South was called to confront; and it was Lincoln's consummate generalship, happily for the South, that held these radical and aggressive elements in check. From a disciplined army in the field, the populations of the seceding States had far less to fear, even when its soldiers were embittered by disaster or inflamed by success.

The attitude of Lincoln in the contest was that of the famous warrior whose sagacious policy of procrastination baffled the Carthaginian invader, flushed with successive victories over the consular armies of Rome. As it was felicitously said of the one so most fitly it may be said of the other:

UNUS HOMO NOBIS CUNCTANDO RESTITUIT REM.

Abraham Lincoln was, politically, the highest embodiment of the ideas, the aspirations, the impulses of his time. He was the incarnation, too, of the sovereign will which made him chief. Popular clamours wearied his ear and vexed his heart; but they could not affect the convictions of a lifetime, his profound sense of administrative duty, or the settled policy of the pending war. He was leading the forces of the loyal States; he was assailing the forces of the seceding States; he endeavoured to be faithful to the fundamental interests of both. When the end of the Confederacy came, he was standing as a tall, strong pillar of support for the broken and exhausted South; and when he fell, the vanquished Confederates felt that their cause was indeed lost. They looked forward to the inauguration of his successor with a natural sentiment of dread. This sentiment of apprehension was not realised at once. Though an iron policy of reconstruction was subsequently adopted in the subjugated States, they were happily relieved from immediate apprehension by the heroic interposition of Grant. It is, nevertheless, true that at this particular juncture "the South had lost her best friend." And many a generous Southerner grieved honestly for the loss.

The echoes of that great battle among the Northern hills have long since died away; thousands of heroic combatants are sleeping their eternal sleep in the peace of Pennsylvanian fields, and the convictions which drove them to conflict no longer dominate the thoughts of men, nor, in an economic epoch, direct the policies of States; but the lesson of the battles that they fought will not be wholly lost so long as the souls of men are thrilled by memories of the charge that Pickett made, or are inspired by the sentiment of the immortal words that Lincoln spoke.

★★★★★★

The still powerful army of Lee was now moving southward—a stricken and shattered host, but as dauntless and defiant in retreat as in advance; with its morale unimpaired, its confidence in its leaders unabated, its military prestige increased.

"We failed, comrades," said Lee, "but it was all my fault."

In anticipation of prospective dissensions and a possible war of recrimination among his disaffected chieftains, he had requested General Pickett to suppress, or withhold, a part of his official report. Pickett complied promptly and without complaint. He simply lamented the wanton destruction of his pliant command and the absence of the two brigades whose presence in the battle would have absolutely assured success. Before leaving Virginia, he had said to General Lee that he wanted a complete division; since as much would be expected of a weak division as of a strong one. But, even now, fresh from the disastrous field, there is no diminution of confidence in the intrepid leader or in his staunch and splendid command. Writing to General Pickett, a few days after the battle. General Lee says:

> I still have the greatest confidence in your division, and feel assured that, with you at Its head, it will be able to accomplish any service upon which it may be placed.

The subsequent history of the division shows that this was not merely the formal commendation of a military order or report. The applause of his own comrades was not less grateful than the commendation of Lee. After the battle, says Colonel Fremantle (an English officer who witnessed the charge), the plucky Confederate cannoneers were open in their admiration of the advance of Pickett's superb division, and of the skilful manner in which Pickett led the assault. But there was no applause more generous than that of the men who repelled the apparently resistless advance.

General Hancock said:

> The lines were formed with a precision and steadiness that extorted the admiration of the witnesses of that memorable scene.

General Hunt said:

> The enemy advanced magnificently, unshaken by shot and shell.

The gallant General Hays said:

> The march was as steady, as if impelled by machinery.

Colonel Hall said:

> The perfect order and steady, rapid advance, gave the line the appearance of being fearfully irresistible.

Many impulsively expressed their admiration even as they braced themselves against the impending assault; and "Magnificent!" was the utterance of many warrior-lips that closed and spake no more. "Magnificent!" is still the exclamation of all who read the deathless story of that day. The heroic Lee, with all his outward calm, seemed to be profoundly stirred, and hastened without staff or other attendants to the front, looking as if he would personally rally the broken columns to a supreme and desperate defence. Alexander, the bold artillerist who launched the column, says:

> No soldier could have looked on at Pickett's charge and not burned to be in it.

And what a cloud of witnesses hovered over the scene—a lowering cloud charged with latent fires and ready to burst upon the field below. A camp-rumour had stirred the Confederate heart, and apparently settled the question of supports.

"Lee," it was said, "was going to send every man he had, upon that hill;" and every slope and crest of Seminary Ridge was alive with expectation and eager for the signal to advance. Unhappily there was but little concert of action in that long straggling. Confederate line, and there came no order for a general advance upon that disastrous day.

But the failure—was it the fault of Lee? Who shall decide but Lee himself, who assumed the whole responsibility at once? And yet, even Lee's decision cannot stand against conclusive facts; especially where the assumption of responsibility was determined in some measure by a generous desire to screen subordinate officers from attack, to compose the susceptibilities of some, and to repress the savagely critical instincts of others. His motive is sufficiently apparent in his letter to General Pickett. But as a matter of fact it would seem that Lee had done all that he could personally be expected to do as commander of a veteran well-disciplined organisation, to ensure the success of Pickett's assault. Granted that Longstreet's sound military advice, to move by the enemy's left flank, would have assured the desired results, it does not follow that the failure to support Pickett was attributable to any unsoldierly neglect or oversight on the part or Lee.

The general order for attack was well understood; and every man in the ranks believed, and every subordinate officer knew, that under the commander's order to assault, ample provision must be made for a prompt and effective support. It is not possible for the greatest captain to supervise the arrangements of tactical details. A meddlesome disposition in the matter of military administration has been imputed as a reproach to Napoleon himself; and in no other army than Napoleon's, it has been said, would a subordinate officer be held justified for neglect, because of a failure to receive orders from his chief.

An English officer (Fremantle) who carefully noted, while at Gettysburg, the military habits of Lee says it was evidently his system to arrange the plan thoroughly with his three corps commanders and "then leave to them the duty of modifying and carrying it out to the best of their abilities."

On the second day, Fremantle had remarked that General Lee sent but one message and received but one report. It is said that the most remarkable point in Von Moltke's strategic method was the self-restraint he practiced in giving free scope to his subordinate commanders. Von Moltke might have learned this from Lee; if, indeed, he had not already learned that it is the fundamental maxim of modern administration—select competent and responsible agents and trust the man that is on the spot.

None understood better than the sagacious and experienced chieftains of the South, the absolute necessity of concerted action in that great Northern campaign. Nevertheless, for an apparent lack of that initiative, which is a characteristic mark of the modern soldier, in all ranks, a momentous and decisive assault upon the Federal left centre was allowed to fail. It is possible, too, that the bonds of discipline were beginning to relax; though many thought that in this matter Stonewall Jackson had given the Confederacy a lasting lesson in the early days of the war. When Secretary Benjamin sustained Loring in his insubordination at Romney, Jackson resigned his position and demanded relief from "duty" at once.

But whatever the explanation, the fact remains. The pending campaign was manifestly lacking in concerted action and cohesive force. In the attack upon the centre the Confederate commander applied the final and conclusive test. It was the last battle and upon the last day—the Confederate commander's last desperate play for success. Lee was calm and confident; Pickett was eager and sanguine; and the assault only failed for lack of timely support; lapsing into a spectacular butchery under the astonished eyes of the chivalrous legions of the South. The gallant division had done all that human valour and endurance could do; it had actually pierced the Federal centre, and in defect of promised support, had literally been crushed by the Federal reserves.

But would it not have been better, say the critics, to move by the left flank, as Longstreet advised? No one could be more competent to advise in such a situation than the masterly lieutenant of Lee, a soldier of almost matchless courage, sagacity, and resource. He is sustained, too, in his contention by the accepted maxims or war; by the circumstances of the situation; and by the confessed apprehensions of the enemy, as well as by the declared object and scope of the campaign as originally projected by Lee. If Napoleon operated by the flank in preference to the front, it is certainly no discredit to other commanders to do the same. But Napoleon himself ruthlessly violated the academic maxims of war when he successfully launched Krazinski's squadron of cavalry up the long narrow pass of Samosierra against an almost impregnable position defended by powerful batteries and twelve thousand disciplined men. Energy and genius, says Clausewitz, will easily "rise superior to the beggardom of rules."

The reasons assigned by Longstreet were in a sense unanswerable; nor did Lee attempt to answer them. As Longstreet says, the Confederate commander "had fixed his heart upon the work," and the fighting instincts of every soldier sympathize with the daring commander m this fixed intent. The proposed assault looked practicable to the experienced eye of Lee, and proved to be tactically successful even as delivered by Longstreet's reluctant hand. The Virginians had done all that they were commanded to do; they had captured the enemy's works. That they could hold the works against an entrenched force of thrice their strength, the most sanguine had not ventured to predict. If Pickett could have stayed where he planted his flag, Lee would have completely realised the object of the assault; he would have had full command of the elevated ground beyond the point of attack, and with abundance of ammunition for the artillery, the position would have become the point for a still more successful advance.

The important point "beyond" was Culp's Hill, where rested the Federal right. It was one of the characteristic miscalculations of this campaign that Ewall's assault upon that position should cease, before Pickett's assault upon the centre began. But, if we may credit the observations of Fremantle, General Lee was certainly not accountable for a tactical contretemps so disconcerting as this. Doubtless the most judicious military critics will agree that the worst that can be said of the great Virginian leader, is simply this, that he had been made overconfident by the loyalty, the energy, and the skill of his generals; by the incomparable fighting capacity of his men; and, as the Confederate commander, by an almost unbroken career of military success.

While the result did not fully realise his reasonable expectations, it cannot be affirmed that in a strict military sense it discredited his judgment or skill. General Hunt, the commander of the Federal artillery, pays tribute to the generalship of the Confederate leader when he says that the Confederates "were almost always stronger at the points of contact." It was precisely here, however, that Pickett's assault had failed. The assaulting column was not strong enough at the point of contact, and was incontinently crushed by the reserves, who, rallying on the second line, recaptured the crest.

But in regard to the great operations of war there can be no one more competent to speak with critical authority (if he can speak without prejudice or prepossession) than the man that is competent to conduct them; and in such a case at least it would be sheer effrontery for a subordinate soldier or a simple reviewer to dispute with the commander of twenty legions. Incontestably, such a critic was Lee himself. After the repulse of Pickett's division, he said in the presence of the English colonel, Fremantle; "All this has been my fault."

On the same day he said to the Confederate general, Imboden, his voice trembling with emotion:

I never saw troops behave more magnificently than Pickett's division of Virginians did today. Had they been supported as they were to have been, but for some reason not yet fully explained to me they were not, we should have held the positions they so gloriously won; (presently adding in an; almost agonised tone), Too bad! Too bad! Too bad!

In the winter of 1863-64 he wrote to General Longstreet:

Had I followed your advice . . . how different all would have been.

The adoption of Longstreet's admirable plan would certainly have ensured that perfect cooperation, which, under any plan, was essential to success. In considering the point in dispute (it is only for an inspired commander to decide it) it must always be remembered that the artillery reserved for the advance that day unaccountably disappeared at the critical moment; that the supplies of ammunition for the available artillery unexpectedly fell short; and that the promised columns of support were, practically, at the proper moment for advance, disinterested spectators of the distant fight. The mere possibility of such complications was certainly not contemplated in the original plans of Lee.

Neither is it to be supposed that the Confederate leader could foresee the failure of President Davis to make a demonstration against Washington coincidently with the Confederate advance into Pennsylvania under Lee. Davis pleaded "impossibility," and the dispatch, which was intercepted by a Federal scout, was a positive inspiration to General Meade. It was an assurance that no peril lurked in the rear. Lee's theory was that even a single brigade, with Beauregard to lead it, had been ample force for the end in view. By a demonstration similar to the one proposed, Stonewall Jackson, with a single division, had paralyzed the movements of an army of 70,000 men in 1862.

The brilliant commander had staked everything upon one bold throw; there was a prodigal expenditure of valour, of skill, and blood, but everything was not lost. The great movement had failed and the tide of battle was reversed; but the Confederate leader was still in condition to effect a masterly retreat and the enemy was too badly crippled to venture a counter-assault.

"Our own line was in disorder," said the brave commander of the Federal artillery, "and in no condition to advance."

In darkness and storm, the Confederate forces silently withdrew from the field that had been made glorious by their arms. The commander entrenched a line from Peach Orchard to Oak Hill, covering the line of retreat, pushed his long column of prisoners, and his military impedimenta to the front and moved his army to the Potomac by interior lines, compelling the Federal commander to seek circuitous routes through the lower passes, if he felt inclined to pursue.

★★★★★★

On the return to Virginia the war was renewed upon the old lines, but with a modification of Grant's favourite method of "attrition." Instead of flinging his disciplined veterans in wild assaults upon the Confederate entrenchments, the Federal commander had resolved to drive the enemy into the "open," if possible, and "make the work of attrition mutual." Lee accepted the challenge and arranged for an immediate advance—placing the staunch and intrepid Pickett at one end of the line, and himself at the other. The initial advance was brilliantly successful. Three divisions of the Fifth Corps recoil under the powerful assault of Lee; and Pickett, pressing his advance upon the other flank, drives Sheridan back to Didwiddie Court-House, where, night coming on, the battle rests, and Sheridan appeals to Grant for help.

At midnight there is an urgent dispatch from Meade to the commander of the Fifth Corps, "Sheridan cannot maintain himself at Didwiddie without reinforcements." Duly warned, Pickett falls back to Five Forks, where he receives a peremptory order from Lee, "Hold Five Forks at all hazards." It was an imperative order to do an impossible thing; and Pickett habituated by years of service to this sort of work, cheerfully accepted the task. "Hatcher's Run," was more defensible, but the order was imperative to hold Five Forks, a low, flat, marshy, wooded tract, softened by the winter frosts and flooded by the spring rains; a clayey soil mixed with sand upon which it was difficult or impossible to improvise defensive works and where the very artillery was floated into position upon a corduroy road actually laid under the advancing wheels, a notably different terrain from the rocky slopes at Gettysburg.

Having ordered Sheridan to be reinforced by the Fifth Corps, General Grant sends a dispatch to Warren:

Pickett's division is developed today along the White Oak Pond, its right at Five Forks and extending toward Petersburg.

Here Pickett formed his line of battle behind a hastily-constructed breastwork, W. H. L. Lee's cavalry on the right flank, Fitzhugh Lee's cavalry on the left, infantry and artillery between; in all not more than six thousand men, under an imperative order to hold the position against thirty-five thousand fresh, well-fed infantry and cavalry, supported by heavy guns. Pickett's cavalry, in spite of express orders to be on the alert, had given no notice of the enemy's advance. The Federal general, Warren, remarked this apathy of the Confederate scouts, and attributed it to a growing conviction of the hopelessness of their cause.

The first attack upon Pickett's position was along the whole front and upon the right flank, which was quickly repulsed; but was immediately followed oy an overwhelming assault on the left and rear. Here the gallant Pegram fell. Warren's infantry corps swept down upon the left flank, while Sheridan's cavalry was engaging the front and right. The effect was simply crushing. Scarcely a trace of organization could be seen. Like Dick Wildblood's cavaliers, the Confederate fighters were without front, flank, or rear.

There was wild confusion; but no serious panic followed the surprise. The grand old division amply sustained its well-earned reputation. Charge after charge was repulsed, and it might have held on until night had not the ammunition failed. Even then they made a desperate stand, fighting hand to hand, and at the last, compelled a rally and a stand on Corse's brigade, "which was still in perfect order and had repelled every assault." General Pickett, as if bearing a charmed life, rode through the whirling storm of battle, rallying and reforming the broken ranks, battle-flag in hand. His men were singing. *Rally round the flag, boys; rally once again*, and Pickett, still waving his flag of battle, joined in the rallying song.

Sheridan's men rush tumultuously over the crumbling parapet, and plunge into a deadly hand-to-hand fight. The combatants were so closely intermingled that for a time (says General Grant) it was almost a question which one was going to demand the surrender of the other. Though outnumbered five to one, the Confederate soldiers fought desperately until night fell upon the disastrous field, closing the bloody scenes of the last great battle of the South. Again the Confederate commander stands alone; and again the reinforcements arrive too late to reinforce—even with hope. The glorious leader, though the last to leave the scene of conflict, was not quite alone. As he rode from the ghastly battlefield, a band of devoted followers in slow retreat, drew upon themselves the enemy's fire. They did it to save their commander's life!

General Humphreys, the Federal Chief of Engineers says:

It has always seemed to me, to have been a grave mistake to require General Pickett to fight at Five Forks.

He should have been placed where he could be promptly reinforced from Lee's right. At Five Forks he was hopelessly isolated.

On the morning of April 2nd, the Federal Sixth Corps broke the Confederate line of defence at a point southwest of Petersburg, and A. P. Hill was slain. The lean, grey lines were breaking fast; their gallant commanders were falling one by one; and the proud Confederacy was at last beginning to crumble under the ponderous hammer or Thor.

General Longstreet says that George E. Pickett's greatest battle was really at Five Forks. His operations, he declares, were masterly and skilful, and, if they had been executed as he designed them, there might have been no Appomattox; that if any soldier could have snatched victory from defeat, it was Pickett, and that it was cruel to leave that brilliant and heroic leader, as at Gettysburg, without reinforcements or support. The casualty list of the battle bears eloquent and impressive testimony to the desperate character of the defence. Longstreet says:

He lost more men in thirty minutes, than we lost from all causes, in the recent Spanish-American war.

The unsupported veterans had been butchered in a sort of strategic battue in which brigades were trapped and slaughtered instead of beasts. There followed a crashing echo of this bloody conflict at Sailor's Run, after which (as the biographer happily remarks) there occurred the first reunion of the Blue and the Grey: Sheridan's soldiers shared their rations with Pickett's men.

The military situation in the South during the past three months had become so critical that General Lee and President Davis urged the adoption of a measure which had been proposed in 1862; which had been favoured by General Pickett in 1863; and which had been warmly advocated in the Confederate Congress in the winter of 1865, to wit: The emancipation and enlistment of the slave.

The proposal was peculiarly offensive to the non-slaveholding whites of the South, and the measure, as recommended by General Lee and the Confederate Executive, was rejected in the popular branch. But the necessity for some strong and effective measure was pressing, and the legislative body finally proposed to meet the exigency—the immediate demand for new armies—by the incredible *chinoiserie* of proclaiming a dictator and adopting a new flag.

Within sixty days from that time the broken and dispirited army of Lee surrendered to Grant at Appomattox Court House, Lee having less than ten thousand effective soldiers in his ragged and famished ranks.

In summing up the characteristics of George E. Pickett as a soldier, it may be said that he perfectly realised in his brilliant military career the Napoleonic conception of *un grand homme de guerre*, a phrase which Napoleon sometimes saw fit to apply to a marshal of the armies of France. He was in truth, "the perfect soldier" which Lincoln hoped that he might be; he was the incomparable soldier of Longstreet; he was the great soldier and *paladin* of McClellan, who generously characterised him as "the best infantry soldier developed by the war."

There is an old French proverb which says that *a great warrior must be a sleuth-hound in assault, a wolf in pursuit, a wild boar in defence;* which is merely a medieval way of saying that the true soldier is an embodiment of all the qualities that give success in military operations: "initiative," promptitude, audacity; endurance, stubbornness, inbred Satanic grit; above all, he must have an infallible *coup d'oeil*, or eye for war. As Sovoroff's maxim puts it briefly and characteristically, "*A correct eye, rapidity, dash,*"—the other qualities being assumed to exist. In a battle, as in a boxing-match (to compare great things with small), it is the eye that determines the result. Instinctively, it detects the opening, and, almost involuntarily, it directs the blow.

George E. Pickett was a soldier to the manner born, his biographer says:

A military bent of mind was hereditary in the Pickett family.

The very surname, a familiar variant of an ancient Norman form, attests the existence of a certain Berserker quality in the blood; and this combative instinct was notably manifest in the Virginian scions of the original English stock.

★★★★★★

The military lists, preserved at Washington, show that the Picketts of Piedmont, Virginia, were fighters as far back as the "Old French War" (*Va. Mag. Hist.*). They fought in the war of the Revolution; in the war of 1812; in the war with Mexico; in Cuba; in the Civil War; and one of the same stock, as we have seen, was uncommonly willing to try conclusions with the British Empire on the island of San Juan. They are known in Virginian tradition as "the fighting Picketts of Fauquier" (*Greene's Historic Families*): Not Tybalt's, however, nor truculent tavern-brawlers; but in war, or peace, a grave, silent race—men of reserved manners, simple habits, pacific inclinations, and quiet tastes.

★★★★★★

Thanks to Abraham Lincoln the young Virginian received at the National Academy a training in perfect keeping with his tastes. In the Mexican campaign the young soldier showed at once the stuff of which he was made. The daring exploit at Chapultepec was the beginning of a brilliant career. In the Indian war that followed he maintained the reputation he had won in the Mexican campaign; and added largely to it, in the estimation of scholars, by studying in the occasional lull of conflict the dialects of the various tribes he was called upon to fight; and so strong was the linguistic penchant that came with his blood that he actually translated the Lord's Prayer into the Indian tongue, and patiently impressed it upon Lo's untutored mind.

Nor meantime was he idle in the field. He actively participated in a two years' campaign in which fourteen hundred regulars and two thousand volunteers effectually subdued the savage tribes upon the Pacific coast, the Filipinos of their day. We next see him standing for the imperial interests of his country upon the island of San Juan. His seizure of that disputed territory was executed, as McClellan says, "by a masterly movement in the night,"—anticipating the arrival of the British fleet just forty-eight hours. At "Camp Pickett," a fortified post on the island of San Juan, he continued in command until the beginning of the Civil War. We have followed him through his Virginian campaigns and found him everywhere exhibiting the same high qualities for command.

At Fair Oaks, a Confederate general, in undue haste ordered a retreat under fire. "Pickett, the true soldier," says Longstreet, grasping the situation at once, wholly ignored the order, pressed the enemy harder, and fought the apparently failing battle to a brilliant and successful finish. At Gaines' Mill he signally defeated Casey's division; at Fredericksburg he urged an assault upon Franklin's flank, and effectively answered the enemy's fire at the south angle of Marye's Hill; unsupported by the authorities at Richmond, he repelled the advance of Butler and his 30,000 men; he recaptured the outer line of breastworks at Bermuda Hundred; he saved the town of Petersburg, "the citadel of the Confederacy;" and prolonged the existence of the Confederacy itself.

It was at this time that Grant telegraphed to Lincoln:

Pickett has bottled up Butler at Bermuda Hundred.

This pointed telegram became at once a popular epigram. It stung the ambitious warrior of Bermuda Hundred to the quick. After the war, Butler intrigued to try Pickett by a military commission "organised to convict;" General Grant not only interposed for the protection of Pickett, but offered him the marshalship of the State of Virginia which he declined. The Confederate veteran was "poor and broken," but he keenly realised the difficulties of Grant's position as well as of his own.

"You cannot .afford to do this," said Pickett, "and I cannot afford to accept it from you."

"I can afford to do as I choose," said the generous Soldier-President. And so it passed.

General McClellan has said that:

Pickett was the purest type of the perfect soldier; that his mind was large and capable, and his courage of that rare proof that rose to the occasion, and his genius for war so marked that his mind worked more clearly under fire than even at the mess-table or in the merry bivouac, where his perfect breeding as a gentleman made him beloved by his friends. No man of his time was more beloved of women and of men.

There can be no higher praise than this; not the praise commended by the old Campanian bard,—*laudari a laudato viro*,—but the applause of one who, worthy of all praise, was as fit to bestow as to receive it. It is no slight tribute to this modest and matchless Soldier of the Civil War, that he should take captive the affections of the men he fought, and receive countless proofs of the devotion of such admirers as Lincoln, McClellan, and Grant. In spite of military hardships that would have racked a frame of steel, and of shocks in battle that only a' dauntless soul could endure, the "Bayard of the Confederacy,"—the hero of Chapultepec, San Juan, Gaines' Mill, Gettysburg, and Five Forks,—for a decade of peaceful and honoured years survived the desolating war which gave him a deathless name. The speech of the veteran warrior in the old tragedy might well have fallen from this Southern soldier's lips:

For I have fought where few alive remained.
And none unscathed.

✶✶✶✶✶✶

Before riding into battle on the third day at Gettysburg, General Pickett hastily pencilled a note of farewell to a lovely Virginian girl:

Goodbye and God bless you, little one!

This note was entrusted to General Longstreet, who wrote upon the cover:

As I watched him, gallant and fearless as any knight of old, riding to certain doom, I said a prayer for his safety, and made a vow to the Holy Father that my friendship for him, poor as it is, should be your heritage.

A few days after the battle on Cemetery Ridge, Pickett wrote again to the "little one" in Virginia:

We were ordered to take a height. We took it, but under the most withering fire that, even in my dreams, I could have conceived of; and I have seen many battles. . . . How any of us survived is marvellous, unless it was by prayer.

A few days later he again writes:

213

I thank the great and good God that he has spared me to come back and claim your promise.

This charming and accomplished Virginian girl lived to describe the battles that Pickett fought. Her book is entitled *Pickett and His Men*. It is full of instruction and charm; it reconstructs the period of which it treats, and gives many glimpses of that idyllic Virginian life, which, even in the midst of war, was still touched with the old colonial grace. There is nothing careless or commonplace in the style and the writer seems to be especially solicitous of fairness and accuracy in the statement of historic facts. The dedication is eloquent and touching:

To my Husband and the Brave Men whom he led.

www.ingramcontent.com/pod-product-compliance
Lightning Source LLC
Chambersburg PA
CBHW032055080426
42733CB00006B/285